THE LIFTED LIFE

THE LIFTED LIFE

Preaching Happiness in an Epicurean Age

Ben Pugh

CASCADE *Books* • Eugene, Oregon

THE LIFTED LIFE
Preaching Happiness in an Epicurean Age

Cascade Books
An Imprint of Wipf and Stock Publishers
199 W. 8th Ave., Suite 3
Eugene, OR 97401

www.wipfandstock.com

PAPERBACK ISBN: 979-8-3852-3705-0
HARDCOVER ISBN: 979-8-3852-3706-7
EBOOK ISBN: 979-8-3852-3707-4

Cataloguing-in-Publication data:

Names: Pugh, Ben, author.

Title: The lifted life : preaching happiness in an Epicurean age / Ben Pugh.

Description: Eugene, OR: Cascade Books, 2026 | Includes bibliographical references and index.

Identifiers: ISBN 979-8-3852-3705-0 (paperback) | ISBN 979-8-3852-3706-7 (hardcover) | ISBN 979-8-3852-3707-4 (ebook)

Subjects: LCSH: Happiness in the Bible | Preaching | Epicureans (Green philosophy) | Keswick movement |

Classification: BV4211.3 P84 2026 (print) | BV4211.3 (ebook)

To the churches of the NG Church Network in Nottingham, who have graciously listened to me as I have tried out on them various parts of the Lifted Life message

Contents

Acknowledgments

As well as with the NG Church Network I have, for years, been trying out parts of this project as papers given at the Postgraduate Research residential weeks at Cliff College. They have put up with a number of very different versions of what I think Western culture even is, let alone what the gospel for it might be.

Introduction

> He has always been there, of course, but now I know he's always there: I always in him and he always in me. It's like the release of dying and going to heaven, except I'm still here. I sat in the car for some time once I arrived back home, soaking up how good this was. It was like a safe haven I've been trying to reach all my life and now finally I'm here and I can know for sure that everything is always going to be alright because I will always be in him and he in me.

THIS WAS MY JOURNAL entry for March 2, 2024 after dropping my daughter off at the café where she works on Saturdays. I was due to preach on the vine and the branches of John 15 the next day and I had been studying the passage for a long time. I had also been writing this book, or prior versions of it, for the previous four or five years. I had been wanting to follow my earlier work on atonement, which threw up clear participatory themes, with something that explores exactly what gospel we should preach to this culture in the light of that. It's like I already had the answer: a participatory, union-with-Christ–orientated message. But I needed to find out *why* that was the answer. I was concluding that our culture was basically a modern, state-sponsored form of Epicureanism. And a big part of Epicureanism is the pursuit of *eudaimonia*, happiness, the good life. What I needed was a reason why a message about union-with-Christ would be the answer to that pursuit of "human flourishing" and "well-being" that we see all around us. I was starting to tie certain threads together. Then, the experience described above, which happened when the book was still only half written, provided a confirmation for me that perhaps there is a good match between the message I felt I had and the culture of the people I was meant to bring it to. After all, I was now, through that union with Christ, in receipt of the very happiness pursued by an Epicurean society. I became, and remain, happy.

That experience turned out to be a lot more than just a moment of illumination. It was more than just, "Oh, now I see it." That very evening, I said to my wife, "I feel like I've been born again, again." I had been taking medication for high blood pressure, but my blood pressure lowered instantly. It was like the "second conversion" described by William Boardman, the founder of the "Higher Life" movement—and I was moved to acquaint myself much more deeply with Higher Life and Keswick teachings. My experience also had some resonances with the experiences described in John Wesley's *Plain Account of Christian Perfection*, which I also read with renewed interest. In the months that have elapsed, the emotions have settled down somewhat, just like they did in the wake of my first conversion when I was nineteen. But there have been times when I have felt more joy than I thought was possible. And even when the joy is not so strong, there is a steady, unshakable happiness, like the Epicurean aim of *ataraxia*, imperturbableness.

I hesitate to define my experience as sanctification. In fact, there are some days when I am just as amazed by how *little* I've changed as I am on other days by how *much* I've changed. In fact, I have wondered whether the big mistake was that so many holiness teachers defined this deeper experience as "entire sanctification." The terminology was unpopular because it could generate either disappointment or dishonesty when it was found that the experience did not, after all, eventuate in a life of "perfection," however that was defined, and because it could create two classes of Christian: the haves and the have-nots, the holy and the not-so-holy.

William Boardman's description is hard to beat. He called it a "deeper work of grace, a fuller apprehension of Christ, a more complete and abiding union with him than at the first."[1] And I

1. Boardman, *Higher Christian Life*, 48.

think this is potentially good news to a world so lacking in real peace and joy. I'll be suggesting that maybe our mistake in the past has been to view these "second" blessings and deeper works as something reserved for those who are already Christians. Maybe this "more complete and abiding union" is meant to be that complete and abiding from the very start.

And so, here it is. In chapter 1 I try to define the culture and explain my reasons for arriving at the term *Epicurean*. I then explore the aspects of Christian tradition that have the most to say about a participatory concept of what faith in Christ is and what Christ came to achieve: the Orthodox and their doctrine of theosis, the Catholic mystics and their understanding of the unitive state, and the various holiness and higher life ideas that emerged from eighteenth- and nineteenth-century evangelicalism. After that, I try to weave these three strands together and see where the one corrects the other, and with this combined picture of what Christian experience and teaching has done with the mystical union with Christ, I set out on an expository journey through Scripture. This results in four worked examples of expositions of biblical passages that can serve either as stand-alone sermons or as a series of four teaching sessions, to be made use of as you wish.

May this book stimulate faith that there is more, faith that there is a fuller and deeper work of Christ available.

All for Christ and Christ for all.
New Year 2025

1.

What Is Western Culture?

When we preach, we are mostly not preaching on the streets. Contact with this culture that we call our home is mostly indirect. We meet it in the weary faces of those in our congregations who are all, in various ways, engaged in a complex negotiation between the kinds of norms we their preachers and teachers are offering them from the biblical world, and the kinds of norms they are mostly surrounded by for the rest of the week. And we too are surrounded everyday by countless suggestions, some of which are historically indebted to the Christianity that still influences Western cultures, and some of which are the result of strenuous efforts to unseat those Christian ideals. The Christian influences put us at ease one minute, while the counter-Christian mantras make us feel like missionaries the next. Then, there are many things that could be one or the other, but we can't tell. It would be so much easier to be sent into a culture that we know to be utterly foreign, but whose values we have been trained to understand. We go into it expecting everything to be different and in some ways hostile to the message we have been sent to preach. We get ready for the cross-cultural challenges that lie ahead. It is far harder, I think, to try to embrace a sense of being sent as a missionary to our own culture. The peculiar and unique blend of *sympathy for* and *antipathy towards* Christianity can leave us feeling rather stuck. It is a struggle at times to pin down exactly what Western culture is—even before we get around to recognizing that most Western cultures have now become host to a huge number of foreign cultures that are at various stages of integration.

So just what is Western culture? The fact that this simple question baffles us explains the endless round of Christian paperbacks that seek to categorize the culture as Gen X, Y or Z, as being all about "dualism," "pluralism," "consumerism," "individualism," or "postmodernism," or as having transitioned to "post-Christendom," or plagued by a "sacred-secular divide" or as just plain "secular." Since the late 1990s and the sudden awakening to the new realities of postmodernism (largely thanks to Brian McLaren), there has been a cottage industry of Christian writers helping us put a label on what we see around us. None of the terms quite fit, of course, so there tend to be various provisos, such as the caveat that, though we are in postmodernity, there are still some features of modernity clinging on, and though we are in post-Christendom there are still some vestiges of Christendom holding on for dear life. Then there is the confusing claim of Radical Orthodoxy that the postmodern turn ought to have brought about a golden post-secular age. Yet, the demon of secularity has clung voraciously to power, so it is the work of theology to finish the job. And this it will do not by being postmodern itself, but by recovering its own pre-modern roots in people like Aquinas and Augustine. This, seemingly, will enable theology to take its rightful place once again as the queen of the sciences with the right to have something to say about everything.

By way of clearing the ground, before I introduce my own "ism," it is worth noting that cultural trends that we might want to categorize as something new have an exceedingly long history. As you will see, I am even quite happy to use some of the annoying terminology, but I want to frame things differently. Western culture has, for many, many centuries shown the same recurring tendencies. It is by understanding these deeply entrenched habits of mind that we stand a chance of understanding just what we are addressing from our pulpits, and just what message might be received as genuinely good, joyful, gladdening news to those variously embedded in and wrestling with this culture.

The recurring tendencies of our culture seem to be three.

INDIVIDUALISM

Western individualism may ultimately have its roots as far back as the third-century philosopher Plotinus and his ideas about the flight of the alone to the Alone. In his *Enneads,* the Platonic mystical journey away from the allurements of the world was a profoundly solitary quest. The writings of Plotinus got into the hands of Augustine and helped him along his journey from the strange beliefs of the Manichees to the point when he finally accepted the Christian faith of his worried mother. However, Plotinus's Neoplatonism was more than a stop along the way for Augustine. He consciously incorporated aspects of the solitary quest for God. His intensely introspective *Confessions* gives to history the first example of a relationship with God conceived in purely individual terms. There is no "we" in it—or not much. And it would be Augustine's *Confessions* that were deeply formative for Rene Descartes, and which inspired the Cartesian thought experiment in which he locked himself away in a room, sat next to a stove, while deliberately doubting everything that could be doubted in the search for an entirely assumption-free basis for knowledge. Descartes's "I think, therefore I am" saying was pointedly not "*we* think." Thinking and being were conceived of in unquestionably solitary terms.

When the supposedly "postmodern" age dawned, many Christians were ready to applaud the dismantling of the Enlightenment project and hoped for a post-secular age to dawn in which diverse avenues to knowing, such as intuition, emotion, and even revelation, might gain credibility once more, and maybe individualism too would be overturned.

Sadly, if the postmodern age ever did fully dawn, it ended up resulting in an even deeper preoccupation with the self. The postmodern turn, by making truth entirely subjective—you have your truth, I have mine—accelerated the quest for an authentic personal identity.

This takes us to another story within this story: the story of the soul-searching quest to find ourselves. It began with the Romantic poets and was originally a bourgeois pursuit, a preoccupation for Coleridge, Wordsworth, and Byron. In those days, the much more pressing daily need to put food on the table held such pursuits in check for most people, but this changed in the twentieth century with the consumer culture of the postwar economic boom. Since then, the quest for self-actualization has become pervasive. In fact, with the advent of new debates about what a person "identifies as," we seem to have gone from trying to find ourselves to trying to create ourselves. Individuals alone have the right to decide who they are. This is just a further unfolding of the individualistic trait in Western culture.

When people do turn to spirituality or religion, they do so in an intensely self-oriented way. The research of Paul Heelas and Linda Woodhead in Kendal, England, in the early 2000s brought telling results.[1] Their study found that the forms of religion and spirituality that were growing in Kendal were those that presented people with subjective spiritual tools from which they can pick and choose. The people were seeking a pathway to wholeness. Forms of Christianity, therefore, that offered tools for the healing of one's inner being, rather than summoning allegiance to a set of dogmas, were showing the most resilience. However, despite the way this has been good for some expressions of church, Heelas and Woodhead's conclusions were not optimistic. Their explanation for their findings was "subjectivization," the massive turn towards the interests of the self. In the words of the title of a *Sunday Telegraph* article reporting on the Kendal Project, people are "Really, Really Spiritual, that is, Totally Selfish."[2]

My point is that the newer forms of individualism that have got Christian writers so busy are nothing new at all, but an ancient character trait of our culture that has grown and taken new

1. Heelas and Woodhead, *Spiritual Revolution*.
2. McCartney, "They're Really, Really Spiritual—That is, Totally Selfish."

forms but not essentially changed. Self-determination is king and is probably here to stay.

MATERIALISM

As we shall see, a materialist metaphysic can be traced at least as far back as Epicurus, but the story of its total dominance as a worldview dates to the early modern era and thinkers like John Locke and Thomas Hobbes. Thanks to Kant, a consensus eventually emerged that we do not have the competence to know anything about transcendent realities. Not many would dare to say that such a realm does not exist but there was agreement that it lay beyond the pale of scientific method, and as the scientific method grew into an all-pervasive way of looking at the world, anything that did not lie within its competence became either unimportant or the subject of science's "promissory note" that one day all mysteries will be seen to have a "perfectly natural explanation."

The journey to dominance for the materialist outlook was not a straight line. Humanity seems to instinctively chafe at the flattening out of the cosmos. People struggle to accept a totally disenchanted universe. There were ebbs and flows. The Romantic movement of the late eighteenth and early nineteenth centuries was a reaction against the dehumanizing effects of the Enlightenment and the way the resulting Industrial Revolution had consigned people to drudge-work in factories and live in slums. It offered a brief reprieve for faith. The Romantic turn was not necessarily Christian, but it was not materialist. It embraced first a Berkeleyan and later a Hegelian idealism in which all the world and all of history was being orchestrated by an intelligence, a universal spirit.

However, science had not been dormant, and Darwin's *On the Origin of Species* of 1859 had a disquieting effect on faith, a faith that in many cases turned out to be unexpectedly fragile. For this reason the Victorian era, for all its churchgoing, is often referred to as the Age of Doubt. The stage was set for another materialistic advance. This took the form of the Logical Positivism of the 1920s. Come the mid-twentieth century, it was clear that, after all the soppy romanticism of the nineteenth century, cold, hard logic and scientific methods were making a comeback. But, just like the factories and slums of the industrial revolution which resulted from the first great surge in empirical thought, so now, in the bloodiest century in history, the results of science were proving to be not an entirely unalloyed good. The Nazis had been highly scientific.

In the late twentieth century, part of postmodernity's attempts at dismantling the Enlightenment project consisted in questioning the worth of scientific progress in the wake of two world wars. "Science and progress" therefore was the "metanarrative," or big story, that Jean-Francois Lyotard had in his sights when he wrote the famous words, "I define the postmodern as incredulity towards metanarratives."[3] His criticism was that the scientific method had established itself as an all-encompassing, taken-for-granted worldview, exempt from scrutiny, when it was just a story like any other story. Despite the incredulity of French postmodern philosophers, since then our faith in science has grown stronger than it has ever been. Breakthroughs in neuroscience, genetics, and AI have left us breathless once more.

Materialism, for the average person, is never likely to fill out the worldview picture completely. Most people prefer to keep the door ajar on some other dimension out there somewhere. Yet there is no confidence that we would know what to make of it if we encountered it, so the transcendent realm is kept out of mind nearly all the time.

RELIGIOUS INDIFFERENCE

Even given the previous two traits, there is something far from obvious or self-explanatory about the complete lack of interest in such a fundamental question as "Is there a God?" There is a docile, numb acquiescence that marks a striking contrast with non-Western cultures.

3. Lyotard, *Postmodern Condition*, xxiv.

This apathy or indifference towards faith was, Aaron Edwards[4] has pointed out, perfectly encapsulated in the slogan that could be read on the side of buses all across the UK over 2008 and 2009, and promoted by Richard Dawkins: "There's Probably No God. Now Stop Worrying and Enjoy Your Life." The telling word is "probably." It implies that the question of God is so irrelevant that it is not even worth seriously asking. This slogan is, according to Edwards, symptomatic of a culture that has become deeply "incurious"[5] about faith. Meanwhile, people in most countries of the world are, of course, far from indifferent to faith and seem to be becoming more, not less, religious.[6]

Part of the problem may lie in the fact that secular culture has shown a remarkable ability to assimilate and replace Christian ideas. As a result, our message seems to be offering what people already have. Assimilation has a long history, going at least as far back as Auguste Comte and his brand of humanism. It centers on a strategy of deliberately replicating and hence replacing every distinctive element within historic Christianity. Comte even started his own humanist church, and he would not be the last to attempt that. It is assumed, in any case, that the true end point of Christian morality has now been realized in the form of a tolerant, humanistic utopia governed by secular reason.[7] The point is that there is a process by which Christianity *becomes* secularism. As a result of that process all the unique claims of Christianity start to sound irrelevant, surplus, or outmoded. Christian faith is displaced rather than denounced.[8] Looked at more positively, we can even say that

4. Edwards, "Secular Apathy," 418. See also Aston, "United Kingdom."

5. Edwards, "Secular Apathy," 431.

6. Though the analysis is somewhat dated now, the trends identified by Casanova have continued in ever new forms. See Casanova, *Public Religions in the Modern World*, 3–6.

7. E.g., Milbank, *Theology and Social Theory*, 9–10. Secular sociology "fulfils the destiny of Christianity."

8. A process attributed by De Lubac to the influence of Ludwig Feuerbach's *Essence du christianisme* (*Essence of Christianity*) of 1841, and to Auguste Comte's *Cours de philosophie positive* (*Course of Positive Philosophy*) of 1842. See De Lubac, *Drama of Atheist Humanism*, 171.

secularism is the product of Christianity's success; it takes shape where centuries of Christian influence have become so embedded they are part of the culture itself. The ethics of Christianity are retained and developed. They grow into things like equality, diversity, and inclusion, all values far from obvious to cultures lacking our Christian heritage but somehow self-evident to us. We develop these Christian vestiges into such advanced forms that all the religious and theological elements seem no longer needed, and collective amnesia prevails about where these values originally came from. Sometimes they are even weaponized against the very religion that birthed them.

In fact, a generalized resentment towards Christianity and suspicion of religion explains why this process of assimilation and replacement has progressed a lot further in Western Europe than it has in America. In America, the same alienations are experienced, but the secular rationality by which the country is run is less intrusive and, for now at least, less hostile to faith. In Europe, thanks to our history of crusades, inquisitions, burnings at the stake, and the Wars of Religion, secularism has been fueled by far greater hostility and suspicion. Hence this aspect of the secular is really driven by collective *anti*pathy, even though it has the appearance of apathy.

WHAT IS WESTERN CULTURE? IN A WORD: EPICUREANISM

There is a term that captures all the facets of Western culture we have looked at here: individualism, materialism, and religious indifference. The term I'm using also has the advantage of being about a way of life so ancient that it connects us to the context in which Christianity first arose. It is Epicureanism.

I'm offering this definition as a way to potentially overturn the Charles Taylor *Secular Age* hegemony that has everyone copying his lexicon of technical terms to describe how we got to where we are today. My problem is that, if this is a secular age, then no matter how much we qualify the term by saying that this does not imply a subtraction narrative, it does describe our age in terms of what people don't do. And it leaves us a little daunted. The vast majority of people in large swathes of the Western world, especially Western Europe, are firmly committed in practice to the nonbelief option, as Taylor rightly points out.

But by calling our age the Epicurean Age we are defining people's view of the world in a much less monochrome way, in which nonbelief is not necessarily its all-defining feature. The term *Epicurean* affirms what the culture is, not just what it's not. And by defining what it is we can see more clearly where we could connect and offer good news. And, of course, most people are not consciously or fanatically Epicurean. There is something less monolithic and less intimidating, yet no less accurate as a defining term, about Epicureanism. It really does describe the way people see the world and does so not just because the term happens to fit, but because there is an identifiable historical indebtedness to it via its rediscovery during the early modern period.

Followers of Epicurus (341–270 BC) were materialists. In fact, both the Epicureans and the Stoics were materialists. It's just that the Stoics also believed in *Pneuma*, spirit, which gave life to everything, and they believed in *Logos*, Word, which was the creator and sustainer of the cosmos. Their beliefs were more complex and nuanced than the Epicureans and, unlike the Epicureans, changed over time so that we can identify such things as early, middle, and late Stoicism. Epicureanism, by contrast, was a materialist dogma that changed little over time. Ancient Epicureans believed in atoms, as we do. They were devout empiricists, believing emphatically that certain knowledge of the universe was to be gained only via sense perceptions. Ethically, they were utilitarian like we mostly are, always asking the question: what can promote the greatest amount of happiness and the least amount of pain for the greatest number of people? They were ruggedly self-reliant and individualistic, adamantly rejecting anything such as fate or divine providence that might unseat their unbridled self-determination.[9]

9. Their doctrine of the random "swerve" of atoms protected them against any notions of determinism. See Neyrey, "Form and Background of the Polemic in 2 Peter," 409.

And, unlike the Stoics, they were mostly not religious and indeed, saw religion as part of the problem. They were castigated by the Jewish philosopher Philo for being something very close to atheists, as well as for being hedonistic and holding to a view of the cosmos that was too mechanistic.[10]

Emerging logically from their materialistic atomism was the rejection of the idea of an afterlife. Ideas about facing judgment after we die were, they felt, among the most troubling things we could entertain and the quicker we get rid of such thoughts the sooner we can enjoy an untroubled and happy life. The best solution was to believe that people's souls are made of atoms, just like their bodies, and hence everything disintegrates after death. Epicureans were convinced that religious claims are basically about where you go when you die and that their materialist view of the soul had successfully inoculated them against religion. The Epicurean view of death became so widespread that a common inscription on tombs was the Latin *Non fui, fui, non sum, non desidero*: "I was not; I was; I am not; I do not care."

The Epicureans are mentioned in the New Testament, alongside the rival group the Stoics, as being the dominant members of Paul's audience in Athens (Acts 17:18).[11] The sermon that Paul preaches there has attracted a lot of scholarly interest.[12] For me, it is fascinating because this is the one and only place in the New Testament where we can be sure that Paul is face-to-face with people just like our people: people immersed in a culture of materialism, individualism, and religious indifference. It is there that Paul meets us. Within the Mars Hill sermon, despite Paul's obvious preference for the Stoics (it is one of their poets whom he quotes with approval), scholars have found traces of an appeal being

10. Ranocchia, "Moses Against the Egyptian."

11. Both philosophical schools were founded there at around the same time: 306 BC for Epicurus's "Garden" and 313 BC for beginning of the "Stoa," named after the porch where the followers of Zeno first met.

12. "Probably no ten verses in the Acts of the Apostles have formed the text for such an abundance as has gathered around Paul's *Areopagitica*." Bruce, *Commentary on the Book of Acts*, 353.

made to the Epicureans too.[13] There are also very strong reasons that can be evidenced in 1 Corinthians, that a large portion of the church at Corinth were from an Epicurean background.[14] It could be that much of what Paul says there is meant to correct lingering Epicurean attitudes, especially toward the idea of the dead being raised to life. There is the possibility, too, that there is awareness of Epicureanism in the Gospel of John. Much of the evidence so far marshalled for that seems less than convincing apart from perhaps the more general fact that the concept of eternal life, so central to the Gospel, is deliberately presented as a this-worldly *and* heavenly blessing. The Gospel of John, likely written within a strongly Epicurean context, offers a this-worldly, unperturbable fullness of life of fruitfully abiding in Christ, all described as eternal life.[15]

Similarly with Paul. Though Epicurean rejection of the resurrection is taken on very directly in 1 Corinthians 15, Paul's more common approach was to take on pagan beliefs in a less direct way: borrowing their terminology but outmaneuvering them by offering an alternative vision of life. With this in mind, it may be that Paul's entire this-worldly emphasis—his gospel of a new life of victory, peace, and joy in union with Christ crucified and risen—can be traced *not* to embarrassment over a delayed Parousia (as a whole generation of scholars once taught) but to the need to appeal to Gentile audiences, who were steeped in Epicurean ideals about seizing the day and being happy in the here and now.[16] Not forgetting, also, that Rome and Corinth were likely both hotbeds of Epicurean ideals,[17] and it is in Romans and 1 Corinthians that

13. In particular, they would have shared Paul's contempt for religious superstition. See Schnabel, "Contextualising Paul in Athens,"180–82.

14. Tomlin, "Christians and Epicureans in 1 Corinthians." Tomlin's view has found more recent support in Szymik, "Corinthian Opponents of the Resurrection in 1 Cor 15:12."

15. King, *Epicureanism and the Gospel of John*, 36–50.

16. There is plenty of evidence that the Fathers of the first three centuries did the same: see Jungkuntz, "Christian Approval of Epicureanism."

17. Cicero, writing in 45 BC, remarked that Epicureanism was the most popular philosophy in Rome, and noted the "crowds of arguers" who opposed life after death: *Tusculan Disputations* Book I: "On the Contempt of Death."

Paul presents some of his clearest explanations about the joys of life lived *right now* in union with Christ.

Indeed, throughout the Roman world, the gentiles to whom Paul was sent were more than likely forearmed with materialist answers to his message. Like Christianity, Epicureanism was a missionary faith, and Paul was sent into a world filled with people already prepared to resist him with a well-rehearsed sneer of indifference. It was a philosophy that already had its answers to the human condition laid out dogmatically—the only Greek philosophy with a dogma. And at the heart of that answer was a refusal of the dread of death via a materialist view of the soul, which originated as a reply to Plato's ideas about the immortality of the soul. It was a very anti-Platonic philosophy.

The heart of Epicurus's message was the attainment of true happiness. To achieve happiness, it is necessary to have *ataraxia*, which means "unperturbableness" or freedom from anxiety. Literally it is "terrorlessness." If nothing terrifies us, then nothing stands in the way of us being truly happy. We might be anxious about losing what we have, or we might be anxious that what we have is not enough. Either way, such worries ensure that we are never happy with the way our life is right now.

Epicurus's teaching is best encapsulated in the most important four of his Forty Maxims, which have been helpfully summarized by an ancient follower of his named Philodemus of Gadara, who was one of the victims of the Vesuvius eruption of AD 79, which covered his native town of Herculaneum in molten ash. He summarized Epicurus's Maxims as follows.

1. Don't fear god.

Epicurus says, in his First Maxim, "a blessed and eternal being has no trouble himself and brings no trouble on any other being; hence he is exempt from movements of anger and partiality, for

---

Cicero engages Epicureanism extensively throughout. See also Tomlin, "Christians and Epicureans in 1 Corinthians," 54.

every such movement implies weakness."[18] The poet Lucretius, an Epicurean of the first century BC, showed a lot more passion in his opposition to popular religion:

> Nor is it piety at all to be seen often with veiled head turning towards a stone, and to draw near to every altar, no, nor peaceful to lie prostrate on the ground with outstretched palms before the shrines of the gods, nor to sprinkle the altars with the streaming blood of beasts, nor to link vow to vow, but rather to be able to contemplate all things with a mind at rest.[19]

Epicureans were rarely complete atheists, though they were accused of being so.[20] What they were opposed to what was seen to be religion's "glaring defect,"[21] namely that it was "fear-producing and hence destructive of *ataraxia*."[22] Belief in a divine being, even if this was not of the superstitious kind described here, meant seeing the world as having divine purpose. The side effect of such a belief is to take agency away from the individual, which, despite the apparent comfort of seeing the world as divinely meaningful, actually results in anxiety, according to Epicurus.

2. Don't worry about death.

Epicurus stridently asserted in his Second Maxim: "Death is nothing to us; for the body, when it has been resolved into its elements, has no feeling; and that which has no feeling is nothing to us."[23] Religion was assumed to depend upon the idea of postmortem rewards and punishments to gain any traction. Remove any thought

18. Laertius, *Lives of Eminent Philosophers* X. 139.

19. Lucretius, *On the Nature of Things* 5.ii.1198–1203.

20. Ranocchia, "Moses Against the Egyptian."

21. Strodach, ed., *Epicurus,* 45.

22. Strodach, ed., *Epicurus,* 45. As Neyrey pointed out, in his study of the Epicurean context for the argument in 2 Peter, "The foremost enemy [for the Epicurean] is a judging deity." See his "Form and Background of the Polemic in 2 Peter," 411.

23. Laertius, *Lives of Eminent Philosophers* X. 139.

of an afterlife, and the fear that accompanies it, and the way is opened to *ataraxia*. Human souls, as well as bodies, are made of atoms and are physical. Hence, souls simply disintegrate after death just like bodies.

3. What's good is easy to get.

This could be exemplified from a number of places but is stated most succinctly in Epicurus' Fifteenth Maxim: "Nature's wealth at once has its bounds and is easy to procure; but the wealth of vain fancies recedes to an infinite distance."[24] He keenly observes that so many of us are driven by a dream of much greater success and wealth, yet the longer we pursue these, the more elusive they seem. They are forever deferred. And even those who attain great success and wealth frequently are not content with what they have achieved. Happiness cannot come until that never-ending quest for more is abandoned.

4. What's terrible is easy to endure.

Here is Epicurus' Fourth Maxim: "Continuous pain does not last long in the flesh; on the contrary, pain, if extreme, is present a very short time . . ."[25] He seems to believe that pain is somehow evenly distributed (even though he does not believe in providence or determinism of any kind). Extreme pain and trouble are short lived, but the milder pressures and difficulties tend to go on for a long time. The limited nature of pain is what Epicurus thinks ought to give us every reason not to be anxious. It's a bit like the saying, "What doesn't kill you makes you stronger." Life, with all its unknowns, presents us with nothing to fear.

To continue with the story, then, despite its immense popularity in the middle classes of the ancient world, Epicureanism did

24. Laertius, *Lives of Eminent Philosophers* X. 144.

25. Laertius, *Lives of Eminent Philosophers*, X. 140.

not manage to keep its hold over the popular imagination. And Stoicism, too, with its mild materialistic pantheism,[26] was very soon eclipsed by its much more impressive cousin: Christianity. What held Epicureanism in check was a renewed Platonism, sponsored also by Christianity. In fact, the period from around 500 to about 1500 is probably best described as the Platonic Age. The Reformation is really the overturning of Christian Platonism. Then, in the wake of that overturning, Epicureanism suddenly reappears in the seventeenth century and its atomistic materialism becomes the metaphysical starting point for early modern philosophy. It was the dawning of the Epicurean Age.

This Epicureanization in the early modern era was linked to one thinker in particular. His name is Thomas Hobbes, known affectionately in his day as the Monster of Malmesbury. In his landmark work of political science, *Leviathan*, he tried to come up with an answer to all the conflict of the seventeenth century: the continental Wars of Religion and the English Civil War. His answer was what he called the Commonwealth. The Commonwealth exists on the foundation of a social contract in which an otherwise selfish and brutish population engaged in a war of all against all defer their mutual annihilation by voluntarily submitting to the absolute authority of the state: harsh but fair. The divine right of kings is replaced by a mutually agreed contract between a state and its people.

To get to this conclusion he first advocates absolute materialism. In explaining his position, he gives us his most famous statement, saying:

> The world . . . is corporeal (that is to say, body) and hath the dimensions of magnitude (namely, length, breadth, depth). Also, every part of body is likewise body, and hath the like dimensions. And consequently every part of the universe is body, and that which is not body is no part of the universe. And because the universe is all,

26. The belief that the cosmos itself is, in some sense, divine or an emanation from the divine being.

> that which is no part of it, is nothing (and consequently, nowhere).[27]

His is the first voice advocating absolute mechanical materialism since Epicurus, to whose thinking he owed a great deal. But why is materialism so important to Hobbes? Why does he need this so badly as the foundation for his politics? Because it excludes *religious* authority. By arguing that everyone is a body Hobbes was able to fight back against the lingering remains of medieval Christendom. Now, all aspects of human existence could be imagined as bodily, *never spiritual*, and therefore the concern *only* of the secular state. There was *no public religious zone.*

Hobbes's aim, then, was not so much to secure a basis for scientific method, which so many early Enlightenment thinkers were seeking, but to secure the basis for political order. His was a political materialism, which seems to be a perfect synonym for what we today call secularism. Secularism, at heart, is politically sponsored materialism.

The atomist, materialist turn was not confined to Hobbes. There was a widespread acceptance of this general premise among the early philosophers of science. They differed only in their approaches to achieving certain knowledge of the universe. For John Locke (1632–1704), the mind was a *tabula rasa*, a blank slate. He was convinced, like Epicurus had been, that we absolutely depend upon sense data for everything we can know about the world of matter. He argued that even when we recollect or imagine something, we are only drawing from what the senses have told us and our minds have recorded: "Whence has it [that is, the mind] all the materials of reason and knowledge?" he asks. "To this I answer in one word, from experience: in that all our knowledge is founded, and from that it ultimately derives itself."[28]

John Wesley, the eighteenth-century revivalist and founder of Methodism, was influenced positively by John Locke in the direction of affirming the value of religious experience in Christianity.

27. Hobbes, *Leviathan*, 46.15.

28. Locke, *Essay Concerning Human Understanding* I, i-iv, cited by Brown, *Philosophy and the Christian Faith*, 62.

There is evidence in Wesley of a doctrine that seems to have been developed in response to the empiricism of Locke, something one Wesley scholar has even termed his "theological empiricism."[29] Wesley seems to have believed in a set of spiritual senses that served the equivalent role to Locke's ideas about the physical senses. "Faith," says Wesley, "is that divine evidence whereby the spiritual man discerneth God, and the things of God. It is with regard to the spiritual world, what sense is with regard to the natural. It is the spiritual sensation of every soul that is born of God."[30] The experientialism of the Wesleyan tradition spawned a whole tranche of trans-Atlantic revivalism, and by the mid-nineteenth century, Methodism had become the dominant religion of North America. Even as early as the end of the eighteenth century, one in every thirty English people were Methodists, and one in five of these were active in ministry and leadership, often having come from backgrounds of poverty and poor education.[31] Owing to the pervasive influence of Methodism, the nineteenth century was the heyday of the holiness movement, indirectly spawning everything from the sedate meetings of the early Keswick Convention to the wild proto-Pentecostal gatherings of the Salvation Army, and, eventually, Pentecostalism. Christianity, it seems, had found its answer to the Epicurean turn in our culture: experiental religion. The world was invited to "taste and see that the Lord is good" (Ps 34:8).

The main factor preventing the further spread of experiental religion was the fact that, in our world, in contrast to the ancient world, Epicureanism was eventually adopted as the worldview of choice for the state. William Cavanaugh, in his highly influential article "A Fire Strong Enough to Consume the House,"[32] has traced the story of the emergence of the secular state. He takes us back to Thomas Hobbes and the unrest of the times: in particular, the

29. Cell, *Rediscovery of John Wesley*, 86. See also Outler, *John Wesley*; Mathews, "'Religion And Reason Joined'"; Maddox, *Responsible Grace*; Runyon, *New Creation*.

30. Wesley, "Earnest Appeal." For more on this theme, see Hanover, "Role of the Spiritual Senses in Contemporary Mission."

31. Simson, *Houses That Change the World*, 70–71.

32. Cavanaugh, "'Fire Strong Enough to Consume the House.'"

Wars of Religion, which ended with the Peace of Westphalia of 1648. Cavanaugh observes how, in order for secular politics to be greeted as the bringer of peace at Westphalia, the religious factions supposedly at the heart of late Reformation conflict needed first to be named as "religious," a domesticating and privatizing move that changed the use of the English word "religion" into something we are much more familiar with today. Instead of describing a way of life typically practiced in a monastery, it became a word that describes a privately held set of convictions. The wars that had torn the fledgling nations of Europe apart were now to be called the "Wars of Religion." They were, supposedly, wars about dearly held personal convictions. The secular nation-state, savior-like, with its bureaucratic systems, came along to bring reason and peace, or so the story goes. In reality, Cavanaugh believes, the process of building new secularly conceived nation-states was more the *cause* of sixteenth- and seventeenth-century violence than its cure.[33]

The net result of the triumph of the secular state was twofold. Firstly, the state achieved control over its people: Hobbes's desires were fulfilled. The disciplinary power of the state, with its criminal justice system, could now wholly replace the disciplinary power of the church. Secondly, a resentful and suspicious posture towards religion began to increasingly dominate the Western European imagination, which is still with us today. Cavanaugh even describes religion as having been left in a "punishment corner"[34] by Western European secularism.

The story of secularization, then, is very definitely not a subtraction narrative—the slow but inevitable decline of religious observance and diminished recourse to the supernatural. It entails the rebirth of Epicureanism in the early modern era,[35] and its subsequent adoption by Western European nation states. In contrast to ancient Epicureanism, the political supports that modern Epicureanism enjoys make it tough for even Christianity's best answers to make an impact. Under the guise of neutrality, it willfully

33. Cavanaugh, *Myth of Religious Violence*, 141.

34. Cavanaugh, "'Fire Strong Enough to Consume the House,'" 410.

35. Described in detail by Wilson, *Epicureanism at the Origins of Modernity*.

promotes the materialist, religiously apathetic, and radically self-determining traits that Epicurus gave it. If framed as Epicureanism we can see that materialist atomism is at its heart, which then entails indifference towards eternity and transcendence, which in turn spawns more self-reliance and free choice.

Epicurean metaphysics is founded upon atomistic materialism. Its modern counterpart has added to this evolutionary biology. Both work together to yield a view of the world in which it becomes easy to draw the conclusion that everything is purely natural and we are alone. Upon this foundation are built two great stone blocks, side by side. One is self-determination and the other is apathy towards religion. Both are the logical conclusions of seeing the universe strictly as "body," to use Hobbes's word for it. But we soon find ourselves in the realm of Epicurean ethics, once its metaphysics is clear. Epicurean ethics tends to consist of one overriding concern: well-being. The main benefit of self-determination and religious indifference is the freedom to pursue one's own happiness without a care for fate, providence, or the afterlife. The result is that the pursuit of happiness becomes all-consuming. But this freedom comes at a price, and that price is the absence of a teleology. In other words, there's no point to anything. There is a yawning desire for meaning and purpose. This explains why so many today have thrown themselves behind a cause. Modern culture is on an intensely moralistic journey to try to make life feel more meaningful, but without any fixed criteria by which we might judge that meaning has been achieved.

So, how do we engage with this culture? We should ask ourselves, firstly, where is it closed? First and foremost, Epicureanism is closed to non-natural explanations for things. This is the foundation for the whole system. There seems little point, in the first instance, in trying to use arguments for the existence of God, or arguments about the limitations of science. It is worth bearing in mind, however, that most people are not ideologically committed to materialism; they have merely been conditioned by the culture to never raise their eyes above the purely immanent and concrete world of things, people, and stuff to do.

Also, like its ancient counterpart, modern Epicureanism is closed to any proclamation of postmortem rewards and punishments. The old line, "If you got run over by a bus tonight, can you be sure you'd go to heaven?" surely never was the best way to win people anyway.

Epicures are also closed to any argument for religion as motivating morality. Modern humanists are adamant that religionists do not have the moral high ground and that a morally good life is possible without faith. Just like the ancient Epicureans, today's materialists, humanists, secularists deplore the misery that can be caused by "popular religion" and its guilt-inducing pronouncements about judgment after death. Indeed, many would claim—weirdly in harmony with some New Testament teaching (e.g., Heb 2:15–16)—that it is the very fear of death that exacerbates human tendencies to immoral and selfish behavior.

Where is it open? It is open to empirical arguments. It is receptive to arguments from experience. The old adage that a person with an experience is never at the mercy of a person with an argument is especially true here. And as Wesley discovered, there can be a kind of theological empiricism. There is an "experimental" religion, both in the old-fashioned sense and in the modern sense of the word. Christianity in Western cultures has survived the Epicurean shift largely thanks to its ability to argue from experience rather than relying on dogma. And the experiential approach is alive and kicking in various forms among all the most successful forms of Christianity today, especially the various evangelical streams that so many of us find ourselves a part of.

But above all, I would argue, the Epicurean Age is open to arguments for human flourishing. Epicures are perhaps most well known for their pursuit of the good life. One modern Epicure, Catherine Wilson, has even called her introduction to Epicureanism *The Pleasure Principle*.[36] And, of course, by pleasure true Epicures emphatically do not mean the lower pleasures of mere sensual indulgence. Epicures ancient and modern have been characterized as pleasure-seekers in that lower sense: lovers of fine food

36. Wilson, *Pleasure Principle*.

and wine. But while they do not shun such joys, they are keenest to advocate the higher pleasures of living wise, healthy, well-rounded lives. This is where we can easily connect.

Where is it weak? Epicureanism is weakest in the area of teleology. Epicures are consistently unable to give an account for the ultimate purpose of anything. Lucretius would not even recognize that eyes and hands have a purpose, so committed was he to the idea that things are merely the coming together of atoms, without any organizing intelligence behind them. Modern advocates of happiness and well-being also seem to find purpose a curiously difficult subject to broach. Take the speaker and writer Rangan Chatterjee. He is reputable and well-qualified, and bases all his advice on solid scientific research. Chatterjee recommends three steps or legs to "core happiness": alignment (the inner and outer versions of you line up), contentment (feeling at peace with your life and the decisions you've made), and control (that nothing is able to stop you from making decisions and carrying them through).[37]

This is good advice, but what is interesting is that, even when well-being experts are talking about all things fundamental, inward, and core—not just the little practical life hacks—even when they go deeper than that, they remain locked into considerations of self-determination and the self's relationship to the here-and-now. Being friendly to strangers, for example, is recommended but not for the kinds of high moral reasons we are used to in Christianity. Instead, when the stranger responds positively, we get a dopamine hit that helps us to feel that the world out there is not out of control. We should try talking to strangers every day because it will boost our all-important feelings of being in control. It is as though, in order to avoid straying into beliefs and values and ultimate meaning and purpose, a well-being advocate will even be willing to hold onto quite a convoluted explanation for why a given action might be deemed good. They must stay within the realm of

37. Chatterjee | Which leg of the Core Happiness stool will you be working on this week? ALIGNMENT, CONTENTMENT or CONTROL? Let me know in the comments . . . | Instagram. (Accessed December 6, 2024.)

self-determination, various physical processes, and the practical avoidance of pain. They cannot touch beliefs and purpose.

The way to preach a good news that will be received as good news in an Epicurean context, then, must involve starting where the audience is *open*. We need to engage Epicures with our offer of well-being. This may not sound especially groundbreaking and, arguably, many churches have already been doing that for years. Some youth ministries are derided for offering only a therapeutic Jesus and bringing a message that amounts to nothing more than "moralistic, therapeutic deism."[38] What I'm seeking is a way to make an offer of happiness and peace that draws from some of the deepest strata of Christian tradition and some of the most important claims of the New Testament.

I'm hoping that teleology will also be addressed, but the interesting thing that I have found about the in-one-another union with Christ is that the union *is* the union. The unitive state is the destination. As we'll see in our historical section, the Orthodox and the mystics of the Western tradition saw this clearly but the holiness movements tended to see the union only as a way to get sanctification. The goal of God is described in Revelation as a blissful union between heaven and earth in which he will be our God and we shall be his people (Rev 21:3). If the union is the destination, then entering it means entering the rest of faith, and de-instrumentalizing our lives and relationships. It means finding Sabbath not necessarily in a slot of allocated time but in a person, in Christ himself. But then, out of that union, as we will see from the vine and branches image, there is a teleology. There is fruit that we should look for and cultivate.

One of the most reassuring things about looking at the gospel message through the participative lens is the way that union with Christ has been held to be of central importance across all confessions. Plenty of examples can be found within the Orthodox tradition, among the mystics of the Roman Catholic tradition, and within the holiness movements of the Protestant tradition.

38. A term first coined by Christian Smith, *Soul Searching*, but used most recently by Andrew Root, *Faith Formation in a Secular Age*.

Succeeding chapters will examine these three facets of the Christian tradition.

In doing this survey of the traditions we are starting to investigate whether the cure fits the diagnosis. The diagnosis is that we live in an intensely individualistic age resting on materialistic assumptions, what Charles Taylor describes as the "buffered self" living within an "immanent frame." We are insulated, nonporous individuals who understand the world around us as a purely immanent world with no transcendent realm, nothing beyond physical, concrete, and earthly preoccupations. That such a culture would be religiously indifferent is almost to be expected and, as we saw, even when there is some interest shown in spirituality, it is a spirituality of the individual, a buffered-self spirituality.

All of this creates a need. We have become a people of the absence, not of the Presence, a people of the ache, of the hole seeking to be filled with all that can be consumed, a people of the vacancy which has now been occupied by secular replacements for Christianity, a conceptually Spirit-less void kept that way by the arid scholasticism of our state churches, and ever in need of that strangely Western phenomenon: the revival.

But just supposing our gospel message broke into that subjective world, not by calling people out of it but by a Christ who comes to join them within it, a Word who becomes flesh and joins our human domain and then, through our answering faith, enters into our individual subjectivities. Once there, he sets us free from all the things about our subjectivity that held us hostage to ourselves.

2.

The Orthodox Tradition

Both East and West share in the conviction, clarified by the Council of Chalcedon of AD 451, that Jesus of Nazareth was both fully human and fully divine in one undivided person. In the words of the Chalcedonian definition, Christ was "of the same essence as the Father according to his deity, and the same one is of the same essence with us according to his humanity." This is what we mean by incarnation. And it is about as far as we can go in our attempts to penetrate the mystery of incarnation before we encounter divergences among the different confessions as to the nature of the divine-human union in Jesus of Nazareth.[1] The incarnation means that he who is one with the Father has become one with us too.

What marks out the Orthodox traditions from others is how rigorously the Orthodox have *applied* the incarnation. The two main ways in which the incarnation is applied within the tradition together form what the textbooks call a "theory of the atonement." Writers on atonement theory focus mainly on the concept of "recapitulation," which is an awkward and ugly-sounding word. This is often grouped together with the rather exotic "Ransom to Satan" theory, to produce a general "Patristic" approach to atonement, historically treated by Western scholars, until recently, as a fanciful historical curio. I may have had something of that attitude

1. Neither the Oriental Orthodox nor the Syriac Orthodox accept all the rest of the wording of the Chalcedonian definition.

when I began looking seriously at Patristic models of atonement during the writing of *Atonement Theories: A Way Through the Maze*. But recapitulation especially caught my attention. It is a word that points to the way in which, through the whole sweep of the incarnate Son's life, death, and resurrection, humanity has been given a new head, a new Adam. I noticed how recapitulation goes together, not so much with the ransom to Satan idea, but more with another classic idea of the Orthodox: "theosis," or deification. In fact, theosis is often used as a blanket term that assumes the recapitulation element. It struck me as an inspiring and poetic way of looking at the cross that brings us out of the zone of transactions and penalties yet does not dump us in the zone of exemplary sacrifice and moving martyrdom. It is a framework for dynamically *participating* in the work of Christ. It shows us how to have a *transforming* experience of Christ crucified and risen.

THE STORY OF RECAPITULATION AND THEOSIS

The idea behind both recapitulation and theosis is best expressed in the rightly famous aphorism of Irenaeus: "Our Lord Jesus Christ, the Word of God, through his superabundant love, became what we are so that he might make us altogether what he himself is."[2] Athanasius is similar: "He was incarnate that we might be made god."[3] In fact, phrases like these recur sufficiently often in the Fathers to have earned the term "exchange formula." The exchange formula needs, on the face of it, little unpacking. We immediately understand, at the very least, the poetic beauty of a statement of this kind in the Fathers. We see the symmetry, and how this very symmetry highlights the gloriously asymmetrical element: the fact that the Son has so graciously condescended to us and then so mercifully admitted us into participation with him.

2. Irenaeus, *Against Heresies* V, Preface. Author's translation from the Greek: *Sources Chrétiennes no. 153: Irénée de Lyon.*

3. Athanasius, *On the Incarnation of the Word* 54:3. Author's translation. The Greek: "Αὐτὸς γὰρ ἐνηνθρώπησεν, ἵνα ἡμεῖς θεοποιηθῶμεν."

It's not as though the exchange benefits each party equally, like we would normally expect from an exchange. It is a lovingly *unequal* exchange. Christ abases himself to become us, to represent us, to become humanity-in-person, and then lifts us to be seated with him in heavenly places, our lives joined in interpenetrating union.

Origins

The thinking behind this originates with Platonic thought. This Platonic flavor partly explains why it feels so foreign to us in an age and a culture that has moved so far away from Platonic metaphysics. Before Plato, and contemporaneous with him, there was, in the Greek poets, an idea closely related to theosis. That's the phenomenon of "apotheosis." The term describes the moment a mortal has become such a hero that they are welcomed into the company of the gods. They effectively become a god and can serve as an intermediary between the gods of the pantheon and the world of mortals—somewhat like saints within the Roman Catholic tradition. Apotheosis has been adopted into the English language to describe someone who has risen to the very height of their power and prestige. Such a person is at the very top of their game.

Plato developed this idea of a deifying apotheosis by making the claim that such a profound transformation is an experience open to anyone, not just heroes. He was convinced that we all originated from a heavenly realm in the first place, a place where we saw the true nature of things perfectly. Indeed, he even thought that we all possess an innately godlike nature, which merely needs rediscovering. The soul is "akin to the divine."[4] And it is in a person's rational faculties that they are at their most godlike.[5] To regain their vision of true reality a seeker, therefore, must train the mind.[6] They must take the path of the philosopher—by which he meant something more like what we would describe as a mystic.

4. Cooper's edition. The Greek is: "συγγενὴς οὖσα τῷ τε θείῳ . . .," a relative or sibling, in essence, to the divine. Plato, *Republic* 611e.

5. Plato, *Timaeus* 90.

6. Plato, *Phaedo* 107c-d; *Republic* 611e.

One must take the path of rational contemplation. The result will be that you become more and more like the beautiful truths you are contemplating. The goal, for Plato, was "likeness to God as far as possible."[7] Why? Because he was desperate to get at the true nature of things and he (and Socrates) felt that the only way to do that was to somehow escape this world of change and decay. Such a world only ever presents us with copies, shadows, and deteriorated versions of things, never their unchanging essence. Eventually, according to Plato's Socrates, you could participate in the divine so much that, after death, your soul would become winged (possibly the true origin of the silly idea that when we die, we become a winged, harp-playing cherub).[8] You dwell eternally in the heavenly realm, permanently delivered from having to keep re-entering thousands of years' worth of cycles of reincarnation.[9] The love of wisdom is, hence, the pursuit of disembodied immortality. And the breaking down of the boundary between the divine and the human, in Greek thought, is synonymous with the breaking down of the boundary between mortal and immortal, death being the main thing that separates humans from the gods.

Dissatisfaction with the traditional worship of the gods had begun as early as the sixth century BC[10] and cravings for a more spiritual, deifying path grew steadily, creating the plurality of philosophical and mystic pathways that were available by the time we get to the first century, and which Christianity successfully competed against. The longing was always for union with the

7. Plato, *Theaetetus* 176b. Greek: "ὁμοίωσις θεῷ κατὰ τὸ δυνατόν." This can be translated as "like God in accordance with that part [namely the rational part] that is able." Russell, *Doctrine of Deification in the Greek Patristic Tradition*, 39.

8. Probably via Clement of Alexandria and his reference to Plato in *Stromateis* 4.25

9. Three cycles of reincarnation in which you have managed to live a pure life are what qualify you for this release: Plato, *Phaedrus* 249a. It will take 3,000 years in order to account for the 1,000-year term spent in a nether world between each reincarnation. It's 10,000 years if you've not done so well: *Phaedrus* 248e.

10. John Lenz, "Deification of the Philosopher in Classical Greece," in Christensen and Wittung, eds., *Partakers of the Divine Nature*, 49.

gods, which would procure release from corruption and death, a partaking of their divine nature. I have suggested elsewhere that Paul, in places like Romans 6:1–11, is making at least *some* reference to these spiritual pathways—known as the mystery religions—and their pursuit of union with a deity's seasonal death and resurrection.[11]

Adaptation: Irenaeus of Lyon (120/140–200/203), Athanasius (293–373), and Gregory of Nazianzus (329–390)

The fathers developed their doctrine of theosis by adapting Platonic ideas. The doctrine began with Irenaeus but came to full flower in the Alexandrian fathers (Clement—who coins the term *theosis*—Origen, and Athanasius), of whom Athanasius is the most significant, and then matured in the Cappadocian Fathers (Basil of Caesarea, Gregory of Nyssa, and Gregory of Nazianzus), of whom Gregory of Nazianzus is the most significant.

Many of the fathers, including Athanasius and Gregory of Nazianzus, loved certain of Plato's writings, repeatedly going back to such works as *Phaedrus*,[12] *Timaeus*,[13] and *Theaetetus*.[14] Yet, they were not indiscriminate about what they took from Plato. It was plain that not everything in Plato was compatible with biblical ideas. I will deal firstly with what they kept, then what they took away, and, finally, what they added.

What they kept was the notion that the human soul already was akin to the divine. The human soul is already a close relative of divine nature. In fact, the Greek fathers seemed to hold a view of

11. Pugh, *Pictures of Atonement*, 45–67.

12. Especially *Phaedrus* 250b-c, which describes the blessed clear-sightedness with which human souls were originally endowed.

13. Especially *Timaeus* 90b-d, which describes how the human soul becomes like that which it contemplates, i.e., more godlike.

14. Especially *Theaetetus* 176, where Socrates urges that everyone who would escape evil should pursue the goal of becoming as much like God as possible.

salvation history that Andrew Louth[15] has described as involving two different narrative arcs or stories. There is the great big story of God's plan for the cosmos that always was going to culminate in him uniting himself to humanity, and humanity entering union with him. This was frustrated by the fall, so there is the slightly smaller story (yet clearly immensely significant) of how, in the all-along-planned act of uniting himself to humanity, God was also able to offer, as a genuine human on humanity's behalf, the necessary sacrifice for sin. But the point here is that the Greek fathers who inspired the Orthodox tradition were a lot more convinced than the Western traditions tend to have been, of the importance of the image of God in humans, the importance of original human dignity. They saw humanity as less devastated by the guilt and power of sin than Westerners have, more attuned to the closeness of human nature to divine nature and the possibilities of a union. In many ways this is the key to understanding the whole concept of theosis. It is in the anthropology of Irenaeus, Athanasius, and Gregory that we find the logic of theosis. It is an anthropology of original blessing rather than original sin, which can yet rise to its original godlike goodness and immortality by cooperating with the disciplined process of theosis.

Here is Athanasius:

> For man is by nature mortal, in that he came into being from non-entity; but because of his likeness to "him who is" he would have lived henceforth as God (for that is the meaning of the scriptural passage, "I said, You are Gods . . . , but you will die like men . . .") had he preserved that likeness by contemplation of God and thus blunted the power of disintegration which is natural to him. . . . For God has not only made us out of non-entity but also bestowed upon us a life like the life of God, by the grace of the Word.[16]

15. Louth, "Place of *Theosis* in Orthodox Theology," in Christensen and Wittung, eds., *Partakers of the Divine Nature*, 35.

16. Athanasius, *On the Incarnation* 4–5, in Bettenson, ed., *Early Christian Fathers*, 274.

Athanasius has clearly found in the Genesis account a corroboration of the Platonic notes of humans having been originally created with a nature akin to the divine. We were made with God's likeness.

And Gregory:

> [God] produced man. He took the body from already existing matter and put in it a breath taken from himself (which the Word knows as the intelligent soul and the image of God). This man he set upon the earth as a kind of second world, a microcosm; another kind of angel . . . He was king of all upon the earth, but a subject of Heaven; earthly and heavenly; transient, yet immortal; belonging both to the visible and the intelligible order; midway between greatness and lowliness; combining in the same being spirit and flesh: spirit, because of God's grace; flesh, because raised up from the dust . . .[17]

Gregory looks at humanity through the lens of the *communicatio idiomatum*, the communication of the attributes, which had been at the center of christological debate. This was all about how the divine and human natures coexist in the one person of Jesus of Nazareth. Gregory thinks this is just like the way humans were originally made: all along a mix of dust and divine breath. This prefigures the "new mixing" of divine and human natures that happens through our participation in Christ by faith.

And this brings us to what the fathers did not take from Plato. This too is in the area of anthropology, but requires only a brief word. They eliminated the pre-existence of the soul and the transmigration of souls: "I am afraid of the introduction here of a certain ridiculous theory: that the soul has had a life elsewhere, and after that has been attached to this body . . . ,"[18] says Gregory of Nazianzus, despite the fact that his mentor, Origen, had been quite favorably disposed to these less biblically reconcilable aspects of Plato.

17. Gregory of Nazianzus, *Orations* 45.

18. Gregory of Nazianzus, *Orations* 14.

What is of supreme interest is what the Greek fathers added to Platonic ideas, to the point of making some drastic alterations to the entire Hellenistic worldview. They brought the gracious incarnation of the Son of God right into the center. No longer was participation in the divine nature something attained solely by disciplined contemplation (though asceticism was valued). Christ had first made an astonishing *descent* into human nature, even to the point of dying on a cross. That descent into human nature means that a comingling between divine and human natures has already taken place in Jesus of Nazareth. Our divinization is made possible by his prior humanization. Now all that is needed is an answering *ascent* into the divine. This happens by a response of faith by which, in the Spirit, each particular human is joined to the divine nature in Christ. He is joined to our human natures through incarnation; we are now joined to his divine nature through faith.

Here is Irenaeus at his poetic best:

> As he was man that he might be tempted, so he was the Word that he might be glorified. The Word was quiescent, that he might be capable of temptation, dishonor, crucifixion, and death; while the manhood was swallowed up in his victory, his endurance . . . his resurrection and ascension . . . Eve by her disobedience brought death upon herself and on all the human race: Mary, by her obedience, brought salvation . . . As through a conquered man our race went down to death, so through a conqueror we ascend to life . . . In the first Adam we offended God by not performing his command; in the second Adam we have been reconciled, becoming "obedient unto death" . . . As through a tree we were made debtors to God, so through a tree we receive the cancellation of our debt.[19]

Emerging from this poetic symmetry of ideas, Irenaeus is the very first person to introduce the concept of "recapitulation" into the language of atonement. The Greek word he would have used (almost none of the Greek copies of his works have survived, only the Latin translations), would have been the word that we find in

19. Irenaeus, *Against Heresies* III.19.3; 22.4; V.3.1;16.3; 17.3.

Ephesians 1:10: *anakephalaiosis*, which there describes how everything will be summed up in Christ as the sole head of all things.

Irenaeus uses the word in an interesting variety of ways. It can mean consummation, restoration, concentration, canceling out, reproducing, or re-enacting.[20] All these meanings come together in his understanding of the way Christ, as the second Adam, goes over the same ground as the first Adam, goes through every test and even undergoes all the consequences of the failures of the first Adam, and emerges having consecrated every phase of life, having passed every test and having deleted the guilt and consequences of every failure, even destroying death itself. Its underpinning logic is participation and representation, and it naturally leads to the corollary that is emphasized by Athanasius and Gregory: our symmetrical partaking of the divine nature as reply to his partaking of our human lot.

Here is Athanasius—though using the doctrine polemically against denials of the full divinity of Christ and the Spirit, he offers us a window into how salvation works in his view:

> For He has become Man, that He might deify us in Himself, and He has been born of a woman, and begotten of a Virgin, in order to transfer to Himself our erring generation, and that we may become henceforth a holy race, and "partakers of the Divine Nature."[21]

Here is Gregory:

> He made his appearance as God, with the assumption of human nature, a unity composed of two opposites, flesh and spirit. The former he deified, the latter was already deified. O strange mixture! O marvelous blending! . . . He shares in my flesh in order that he may rescue the image and confer immortality on the flesh. He enters upon a second fellowship with us, much more wonderful than the first. Then he imparted an honour; now he

20. Bettenson helpfully discusses these meanings: Bettenson, ed., *Early Christian Fathers*, 81, 83n3.

21. Athanasius, "Letter to Adelphium 4."

> shares a humiliation. The latter is a more godlike act, and thoughtful men will find it more sublime.[22]

Gregory rejoices in the "felix culpa," the happy fault. He is in awe of the mystery that means we, in this "second fellowship," that of our redemption, have a better lot than Adam and Eve, who had the honor of the first fellowship of creation in the image of God. Thanks to God's gracious action in Christ, the fall, the "culpa," has happily eventuated in an immeasurable blessing.

A factor which, at this early stage in the doctrine, can keep the doctrine of theosis feeling somewhat abstract is the fact that the doctrine tends to be used to prove a point against a heresy. Irenaeus wants to show that Christ really did come in the flesh (he was not a phantom) and that, if this had not been the case, then, on the logic of the exchange formula, humanity could not have been truly deified. Once Athanasius got embroiled in the Arian controversy, he sought to prove that our Savior must be fully divine, and not merely the highest and noblest of God's creatures (the Arian view), since how else could he divinize us? Only a divine being can impart divine life and, because salvation *is* deification according to Athanasius, we cannot be saved if Christ is not fully divine.

Gregory wanted to show the Apollinarians that every part of the human Jesus of Nazareth was divinized by divine nature: mind, will, soul, body. He argues that, because we are divinized *to the same degree* that the earthly Jesus was infused by divine nature, *our* deification would only be partial if *his* was partial. The Apollinarians had been arguing that the mind of Jesus was not a union of human and divine but a wholly divine intellect, the Logos, utilizing nothing human at all. This is when Gregory coins his famous phrase: "What is not assumed is not healed."[23] In other words, only those facets of humanity that were taken up into the person of Christ could have been healed and saved by him. If something has been left to one side, it's not healed.

22. Gregory of Nazianzus, *Orations* 38.13.

23. Gregory of Nazianzus, *Epistle 101 to Cledonius the Priest Against Apollinarius*, in Bettenson, ed., *Early Christian Fathers*, 108.

Profound though these insights are, these writers seldom take the doctrine as a source of edification and unpack it as a thing in itself. It keeps ending up as a polemical tool. As a result, it fails to develop very far beyond various reiterations of the exchange formula, some extended, some brief.

The doctrine did not remain static, however. Over what we now call the Byzantine era, theosis became a cornerstone of Orthodox devotion. A quick look at what the three most important of the Byzantine mystics did with theosis in their devotional lives seems worthwhile.

Devotion: Maximus the Confessor (580–662), Symeon the New Theologian (949–1022), Gregory Palamas (1296–1359)

Maximus the Confessor

"Confessor," in Maximus's name, means that he is one rank below a martyr. A confessor is someone who confesses his faith in the face of persecution but is not martyred. Maximus was of noble birth but became a monk. He was influenced profoundly by the Cappadocian fathers, especially Gregory of Nazianzus.[24] He was unafraid to question things and pre-empted, by several decades, the third council of Constantinople (680–81) by condemning monothelitism, the doctrine that Christ had only one will, which was divine and not human.

Sadly, he was too far ahead of his time. At the time Maximus began to protest against monothelitism, the Emperor Constans II, and just about everyone else as well, thoroughly believed in monothelitism. Maximus was fighting for the doctrine that Christ had a fully human will, just like ours, but which functioned in perfect harmony with the divine will. Christ was fully human and fully divine in every way possible, nothing excluded. For Maximus, the very possibility of a true and complete union between believers and Christ could be jeopardized by monothelitism. It is in the

24. Russell, *Deification in the Greek Patristic Tradition*, 263.

same grain as Gregory of Nyssa's assertion some 300 years earlier that "what is not assumed is not healed." If Christ did not assume, or take up into himself, a fully human will, then that will has not been healed since it lies outside the scope of the incarnation. Such was unthinkable for Maximus. Unfortunately, he ended up having his tongue and right hand cut off as a punishment, eventually dying of complications arising from his injuries.

Before this rather tragic turn of events, Maximus had much to say about theosis, especially in his *Ambigua*, where the union between the divine and human natures in Christ himself is clearly the template for the union of the believer with Christ:

> A firm assurance, he says, for looking forward with hope to the divinization of human nature is provided by the Incarnation of God, which makes man God to the same degree that God Himself became man. For it is clear that He who became man without sin will divinize human nature without changing it into the divine nature, and will raise it up for His own sake to the same degree that He lowered Himself for man's sake.[25]

In his *Four Hundred Texts on Love*, Maximus describes what it's like to experience the reality of theosis:

> The intellect joined to God for long periods through prayer and love becomes wise, good, powerful, compassionate, merciful and long-suffering; in short, it includes within itself almost all the divine qualities.[26]

True to his growing convictions about the fully human will of Christ, working in frictionless harmony with the divine will

25. Maximus, *Ambigua to John* Question 22:28–29. The mutual affecting of the one nature by the other, combined with the distinct preservation of the divine as divine and the human as human, inspires one scholar to use the word "perichoresis," interpenetrating, in-one-another-union, to describe Maximus's understanding of theosis, though she does not marshal any quotes from him that directly evidence that: Elena Vishmevskaya, "Divinization as Perichoretic Embrace in Maximus the Confessor," in Christensen and Wittung, eds., *Partakers of the Divine Nature*, 132–159. An excellent digest of highlights from Maximus' *Ambigua* is Truglia, "Highlights of Maximus' *Ambigua*."

26. Maximus, "Four Hundred Texts on Love" 52.

(based on Matt.26:39), Maximus was convinced that, in principle, the same can become a reality in us: "Because of this, the Creator of nature himself—who has ever heard of anything so truly awesome!—has clothed himself with our nature . . . so that, gathered to himself, our nature may no longer have any difference from him in its inclination."[27] Christ has gathered our nature to himself, securing the most important aspect of that union: a union of the wills. Maximus knew well enough that very often, we just don't *want* to change. We may know that divine help is available but we *choose* not to call upon it. Well, this union of wills fixes that. There is the possibility of there being "no longer any difference from him" in our will's inclination. Christ and I start to both truly want the same thing.

Yet it takes a certain inclination of the will in order for us to enter into this union: "the mystery of salvation belongs to those who choose it,"[28] and "each one who wishes can be transformed by divine grace."[29] But having entered, we rediscover how entirely natural it is for our human nature to have an "inclination to harmonize itself with God who is its cause."[30] It is a harmonizing of wills first perfected by Christ in the hour of trial in the garden of Gethsemane.

Maximus believes that the way to receive the grace of deification is by way of stillness. To receive the experience is to know a loving ecstasy in which the soul finds its Sabbath: "Sabbaths of sabbaths signify the spiritual calm of the deiform soul that has withdrawn the intellect even from contemplation of all the divine principles in created beings, that through an ecstasy of love has clothed it entirely in God alone, and that through mystical

27. *Letter on Love to John the Cubicularius* 404B. Louth's translation. On this see also Ian A. McFarland, "'Naturally and by grace.'"

28. Maximus, "On the Lord's Prayer," 289 in *The Philokalia*.

29. Maximus, *Difficulty 10*. Louth's translation. See also Elena Vishnevskaya, "Divinization and Spiritual Progress in Maximus the Confessor," in Finlan and Kharlamov, eds., *Deification* 1, 135.

30. Anatalios, *Deification through the Cross*, 213.

theology has brought it altogether to rest in God."[31] It is a state of divine "becoming-movement-rest."[32] It is a stillness of the soul that is "transforming."[33]

So, for Maximus, the mystery of the Word becoming flesh (John 1:14) involves a perfect identity-in-difference nowhere more perfectly exhibited than in Gethsemane where the sinless human desire to go on living yields to the higher divine pursuit of the Son's mission. And we enter the divine nature of Christ by way of a similar yielding of our wills. Ongoingly the transformation of deification carries on by way of *apatheia*, the quiet yielding of our souls to the perfect stillness of God.

It is little wonder that the writings of Maximus have, for centuries, been an especially rich source of spiritual food for seekers of a deeper life. His writings are readily available online and significant portions can be found in the Orthodox spiritual handbook, the four-volumed *Philokalia*.

Symeon the New Theologian (949–1022)

Symeon is called the New Theologian because he is ranked alongside John the Evangelist and Gregory of Nyssa, who were the only other two figures in Orthodox Christianity prior to him to be given the honorific title theologian. Symeon built on Irenaeus's theology of the union of God with humanity in the incarnation. On this basis, Symeon advocated an intimate and personal union between each individual and Christ. This union can be grasped right now, and he freely testifies of his experiences:

> [T]hat light appeared to me. The walls of my cell melted away and the whole world vanished. I think it was fleeing before his face. I alone remained, in the presence of the light. . . . I do not know if I was still in my body or carried

31. Maximus, *Centuries on Theology and the Incarnate Dispensation* I, 39. Louth's translation.

32. Louth, *Maximus the Confessor*, 64.

33. Vishnevskaya, "Divinization and Spiritual Progress in Maximus the Confessor," in Finlan and Kharlamov, eds., *Theosis*, 135.

> outside it. I completely forgot that I even have a body. I felt such great joy within me, and it is still in me now . . .[34]

At times sounding like a Pentecostal preacher, Symeon never tired of reminding people that the glories of encountering God in Christ and in the Spirit are not an experience to be deferred until eternity but should be enjoyed here and now. He repeats the exchange formula in no uncertain terms, adding his own characteristic note of drama and emotion: "God wants to make gods out of human beings . . . He wants this so much that he . . . descends and appears on earth for this purpose."[35] In Maximus, the union had been pictured vividly as air illuminated by light, and as iron or a sword plunged into fire and glowing in its heat. In Symeon, despite his being a more flamboyant character than Maximus, the picture used is of the humbler image of a clay pot being fired:

> It [that is, the soul receiving deification by the Spirit] is like a clay pot that has been set on fire. At first it is somewhat blackened by the smoke of the burning fuel, but after the fuel has begun to burn fiercely, then it becomes all translucent and like the fire itself, and the smoke can communicate none of its blackness to it. Just so, indeed, does the soul which has begun to burn with divine longing see first of all the murk of the passions within it, billowing out like smoke in the fire of the Holy Spirit . . . After these things have been utterly destroyed . . . then the divine and immaterial fire unites itself essentially to the soul, too, and the latter is immediately kindled and becomes transparent, and shares in it like the clay pot does in the visible fire.[36]

34. Symeon the New Theologian, *On the Mystical Life*, cited in Hill, *History of Christian Thought*, 108.

35. Symeon, *Ethical and Theological Treatises* 7.598, cited in Russell, *Doctrine of Deification*, 301.

36. Symeon, *On the Mystical Life, Ethical Discourses* 5 & 7, in Goltitzin, *St. Symeon the New Theologian*, cited in Mayes, *Celebrating the Christian Centuries*, 45–46.

Gregory Palamas & Mount Athos (1296–1359)

The last of the great Byzantine writers we will consider, Gregory Palamas, has continued to exert a great influence upon Eastern Orthodoxy, and now that the spiritual treasures of Eastern Orthodoxy are being rediscovered, the West also.

He is most well-known for his favorite prayer technique, Hesychasm, from the Greek, *hēsuchia*, meaning "stillness." This technique, instead of denying the body, elevated it to a central place as part and parcel of the act of worship. The Jesus Prayer—"Lord Jesus Christ, Son of God, have mercy on me"—was recited in combination with various bodily disciplines. Palamas's contemporary, Gregory of Sinai, outlines the physical aspects of the technique: "Sit down on a low stool . . . compress your intellect, forcing it down from your brain into your heart, and retain it there within the heart. Laboriously bow yourself down, feeling sharp pain in your chest, shoulders and neck . . . Control the drawing-in of your breath . . . So far as possible, hold back its expulsion, enclosing your intellect in the heart."[37]

There is definitely a "don't try this at home" element to this: contorting your body until you feel a sharp pain in your chest is probably not the best way to experience theosis, and even the hesychasts warned that these techniques should not be tried without someone on hand to guide. Their tradition is the source of the idea of "navel-gazing," the act of staring at the navel in an effort to push the truths that the mind has grasped into the lower nature where these higher ideas can bring transformation to that nature.

Palamas spent much of his life at Mount Athos, from where he wrote and became well known. Mount Athos was a place of retreat for those who disliked the wranglings of politicized Christianity. No females of any sort were allowed, except female cats (they helped keep the rats down). By the mid-eleventh century,

37. Gregory of Sinai, cited in Jones, Wainwright, and Yarnold, eds., *Study of Spirituality*, 247. Gregory Palamas also has much practical advice about prayer and controlled breathing: "Those who practise a life of stillness 7," in Palmer, Sherrard, and Ware, eds., *Philokalia* 4, 337.

7,000 monks were in residence. Twenty monasteries still thrive there today.

While there, Palamas won (eventually) an important debate. This debate was, in its own small way, the Eastern equivalent of the Enlightenment moment in the West. It was a debate with a thinker called Barlaam, who had been influenced by the rationalistic tendencies already visible in the West, which by now was at the height of its scholastic period. Barlaam was outraged by the claim that human beings could participate in God. Palamas stood vehemently against him. In arguing for hesychasm he was arguing for the continuation of the mystical, participative heart of Orthodox theology.

Thanks to the stand Palamas took, the rational element in theology never became separated from the spiritual or mystical element in the East, and its theology retains that element to this day. The technique of hesychasm was precisely about pushing the mind *into* the heart rather than letting it do its own thing. Centuries later, the famous Russian text *The Way of the Pilgrim* made this even clearer. The bodily element is emphasized as the anonymous author describes the way he was taught the Jesus Prayer. He was taught to say it in time with the rhythm of the beat of the heart, and then to include the breathing, so that "Lord, Jesus Christ" is a series of inhalations in time with the heart, and "have mercy on me," is a series of similarly timed exhalations.

Palamas often used the Mount of Transfiguration, Mount Tabor, as symbolic of theosis. Those who practice hesychasm begin to experience the divine light, the same light revealed on Mount Tabor, yet the traditional distinction between nature and grace is maintained: the faithful do not attain deification by disciplined effort but by a gift of grace. Palamas's reflections on Mount Tabor take him into the Farewell Discourse of John's Gospel:

> For "the glory which the Father gave him," he himself has given to those obedient to him, as the Gospel says, and "he willed that they should be with him and contemplate his glory" (John 17:22, 24).[38]

38. Palamas, *Triads* I.iii.4.

This survey of some of the most interesting insights from Byzantine spirituality—Maximus's convictions about the power of a divinized human will in Christ and in us who are united to him, Symeon's outspoken insistence that the divine light of deification is to be experienced here and now, and Gregory Palamas's insistence that quiet prayer is heart and center of theosis and of the whole enterprise of the study of divine things—have given us a mere taste, but it is enough to allow us to continue on our journey.

CONCLUSION

There are vast spiritual and theological riches in the Eastern Orthodox tradition that only quite recently have begun to be fully appreciated by the West. The differences we can now see are, in some ways, quite stark, and in a way that does not put the Western traditions in the best of lights. We are looked upon by the East as hopelessly rationalistic and arid. Our rational detachment has produced some fine thoughts about the imitation of Christ[39] but this approach, Vladimir Lossky points out, is "foreign to Eastern spirituality, which may rather be defined as *life in Christ.*"[40]

The effect of an Orthodox perspective on the presuppositions of Western thought are brought out here:

> When the notion of creaturely participation in God is placed at the heart of theology . . . the relationship between the natural and supernatural orders, natural and revealed theology, freedom and grace, secular and sacred spheres, is reconceived.[41]

Theosis, with its intermingling of divine and human, unseats the strict dualisms that have made their home in the West for so long. What has happened is that over time the wall, if you like, which separates the material world from the spiritual world in our

39. E.g., Thomas à Kempis, *On the Imitation of Christ,* and Charles Sheldon, *In His Steps* (the origins of WWJD movement).

40. Lossky, *Mystical Theology of the Eastern Church*, 215.

41. Gavriluk, "Retrieval of Deification," 656.

thinking has been moved to the outer limits by our convictions about what can and cannot be known. The wall has become the horizon. Beyond this horizon we have, as a culture, refused to go for some time. We have indefinitely deferred the need to explore the mysterious places beyond the material. Hobbes's Leviathan is the result: a world we've created in which everything is "body." Theosis takes that horizon, reminds us that it was originally only a wall, and then breaks it down.

It is worth noting, too, that not only did we add the filioque[42] but, by some time in the twelfth century, we rejected theosis in the West.[43] We parted ways with the East in both the doctrines that could have helped us to maintain our grip on the dynamic, transformative, and properly spiritual aspects of Christianity. Instead, we have found ways of keeping God and transcendence at a distance. We have a culture that does this because, first, we had a Christianity that did that. We developed churches that kept the presence of the Spirit out and, when it came to salvation, developed doctrines of the work of Christ that reduced it either to a legal transaction or a subjective emotion. The aching hole in our spirituality accounts for the pietisms, revivalisms, and Pentecostalisms that have compensated for this poverty of spirit.

In this context, we need to identify what it is that would be heard as genuinely good news. It has often been remarked that secular culture leaves people profoundly dissatisfied. It is a flattened out, rigidly choreographed world[44] with no second floor[45] in which a long-lost transcendence continues to haunt people.[46] The person

42. The Western insertion into the creed that states that the Spirit proceeds from the Father *and from the Son*, rather than just proceeding from the Father, which, among other things, demotes the Spirit to "third place" as it were, rather than Spirit and Son being sent equally on a joint coordinated mission from the Father (the Eastern model). *Filioque* is a Latin word meaning "and from the son."

43. Andrew Louth, "Place of *Theosis* in Orthodox Theology," in Christensen and Wittung, eds., *Partakers of the Divine Nature*, 33.

44. Pickstock, *After Writing*, 3.

45. Smith, *How (Not) to be Secular*, vii.

46. Smith, *How (Not) to be Secular*, vii.

steeped in an earth-bound material view of everything feels unable to transcend this mindset. They may even admire those who have a faith. It's not so much that they are refusing to believe. Tragically, they have lost the *capacity* to believe.

Our gospel, if framed in terms of recapitulation and theosis, is good news for the person longing to escape a material mindset because it does not demand the impossible. It does not expect the materialist to self-transcend, believe something they find impossible and reach for something entirely beyond them. But unlike the various new spiritualities on offer, our gospel does not leave the seeker stuck in their own inner world either. It brings news of an invasion. God has taken complete responsibility for the alienation and has reconciled himself to us by uniting himself to the whole of humanity in one particular human. In that representative, he has entered the human zone. And it is only because the divine has entered the human zone that our hearers can enter the divine zone.

But, even apart from the spiritual seekers we encounter along the edges of an Epicurean culture, I am putting forward the general idea that a participative view of the saving work of Christ, a participation in Christ—whether we call it theosis or something else—is the right gospel to preach in an Epicurean age. Why?

Let's briefly revisit the pithiest summary of Epicurean ethics, sometimes known as the *tetrapharmakos*, the Four Cures: Don't fear god, Don't worry about death; What is good is easy to get, What is terrible is easy to endure.[47] In Epicurus, the goal (not that he liked to speak of goals) was *ataraxia*, freedom from mental anguish. All four pieces of advice are aimed at helping the reader towards a worry-free life, on the assumption that belief in a judging deity and an afterlife are the principal underlying causes of disquiet in people. And, indeed, a powerless, union-less belief in a God far above me who might arrive at a terrible verdict about my life after I die, is a disquieting belief.

What I am suggesting is a path to *ataraxia* that does indeed involve the rejection of *this* kind of faith. As I hope is already clear, this was never the message that Paul, John, or the Greek fathers

47. Hutchinson, ed., *Epicurus Reader*, vi.

equated with the gospel. Their gospel was the remedy to this, a way to "peace with God" (Rom 5:1), a way to "life in all its fullness" (John 10:10), a "marvelous blending" with the divine Christ.

This chapter has been about learning from the Orthodox but the truths about our union with Christ have been celebrated by Catholics and Protestants too. The Roman Catholic mystics had much to say about the mystical pathway through purgation and illumination and into the unitive state. To this tradition we now turn.

3.

The Western Mystical Tradition

LIKE THE EAST, THE Western Roman Catholic mystical tradition is impossible to understand without understanding the influence of Plato and Neoplatonism. Specifically, Platonic influences gave the spirituality of East and West three enormous areas of emphasis that recur until the Reformation, which brought about a departure from Platonic ways of thinking for the West. The first two emphases were such a good fit for concepts that were already native to the Christian faith that the Platonic spin on them only served to define, enhance, and preserve those emphases. These are the priority of the transcendent realm and the participative view of faith and knowledge. The third emphasis, asceticism, has resulted in distortions of the Christian message, which inadvertently helped to bring about the Reformation.

The Priority of the Transcendent

The transcendental nature of ultimate reality is the one constant of Platonic influence. It insists upon "a higher level of reality beyond the manifest image of the world."[1] Platonism has helped Christianity hold on to the belief that the transcendent and super-sensual realm is actually *more* real than the concrete everyday realities

1. Hampton and Kenney, eds., *Christian Platonism*, 4.

around us.[2] It has helped Christians maintain this belief in the face of the onslaught of philosophical materialism.

Plato's views about the transcendent realm are mostly to be found in the dialogues that contain long exalted speeches, such as the *Timeaus*, which waxes lyrical about the creation of the cosmos. They are also found in *Phaedrus*, which contains a speech made by Socrates to a friend while out walking beside a river about rhetoric and true philosophy—the forms to which fine oratory ought to point. The transcendent realm is the realm of the "forms"—archetypes or prototypes—of which everything in this life is a changing and never perfect copy.[3] As we have seen, Plato (and Socrates) believed that we saw this world of original beautiful things before we were born (an idea especially prominent in *Phaedo*).

Believing as Participating

Plato's quest was for true and certain knowledge, for an understanding of that which "transcends the changing and shifting nature of this world."[4] In Plato's *Phaedo*, a key moment is reached in the dialogue with the simple recognition that "the invisible always remains the same, whereas the visible never does,"[5] which happens to have some resonances with Paul (see 2 Cor 5:7). Christians have shared with Plato the desire to truly see the goodness, truth, and

2. In Platonism, "The higher must explain the lower, and not vice-versa." Douglas Hedley, "Christian Platonism in the Age of Romanticism," in Hampton and Kenney, eds., *Christian Platonism*, 307.

3. The only aspect of this belief in forms that still seems reasonable to us today is the geometric aspect of Plato's quest. He (along with Euclid, Pythagoras, et al.) was convinced that there was an underlying geometrical order to the world, which provides something eternally constant and measurable beneath the shifting sands of time and change. He was proven right. See page 21 and chapter 8 of Thompson, *Christian Spirituality*.

4. Louth, *Origins of the Christian Mystical Tradition*, 2, reflecting Plato's *Republic*, *Symposium*, *Phaedrus*, and *Philebus*. For an ultra-accessible introduction to Plato's theory of Forms, see my "Plato and His Big Idea."

5. *Phaedo* 79a, Cooper's translation.

beauty of God, to achieve the beatific vision through a contemplative act that entails union with the object of faith's desire.

Yet there are vital reasons why Plato's ideas about knowing ended up being such a good fit as Christianity grew in its self-understanding. Here is Andrew Louth: "Knowledge is for Plato more than knowledge *about:* it implies identity with, participation in, that which is known."[6] And even the Western tradition embraced this participative view of knowledge to begin with. In both Platonism and early Christianity, contemplation was understood to be the key to true knowing. Both Plato and the fathers used the term *theoria*, which carries the idea of clear-sightedness, but also of "union with, participation in, the true objects of knowledge," and even, "a feeling of presence, of immediacy."[7]

In the West, especially post-Enlightenment, both faith and knowledge have come to be understood to have reference to a set of things that are the case: believing *that*, knowing *that.*[8] In Plato, it is assumed that the soul becomes the same as, and fused with, the beautiful truths it is contemplating and learning about, since it was originally made of the same stuff. It merely needs to rediscover the world from which it came:

> But when the soul investigates by itself it passes into the realm of what is pure, ever existing, immortal and unchanging, and being akin to this, it always stays with it . . . it ceases to stray and remains in the same state as it is in touch with things of the same kind, and its experience then is what is called wisdom.[9]

6. Louth, *Origins of the Christian Mystical Tradition*, 2

7. Louth, *Origins of the Christian Mystical Tradition*, 3.

8. Today, the simple but profound misunderstanding of what faith is may even be the single biggest reason why so few people in our culture seem to believe. They think "believe" means "a blind act of believing that something (typically seen as far-fetched or mythological) is the case despite the absence of scientific evidence." But in fact, believing all the things that are the case about what Jesus did and who he is comes later. The first act of believing is an act of uniting oneself to Christ arising from a Spirit-imparted awareness of his presence and reality. This is how it was for the 3,000 on the Day of Pentecost, and how it seems to have been in every great revival.

9. Plato, *Phaedo* 79d.

In Socrates's speech in *Symposium*, a similar participative destination is reached. The speakers have been talking mainly about erotic love and the way this is bound up with the desire for beauty. The other speakers are ready to settle for a definition of love that would be something like "wanting to have beauty and goodness." Socrates has something rather more exalted up his sleeve but is characteristically gentle and indirect in his reproof. In fact, he puts almost all of his argument into the mouth of a wise woman, Diotima, with whom he purportedly once had a conversation. It is she, he claims, who opened his mind. Of course, Plato himself is adding his own layer of modesty in that the *Symposium* reflects Plato's own maturing thinking, which is being put into the mouth of Socrates. So, what did Diotima open Socrates's eyes to? She seems to open him up to a hierarchy of beauty. A beautiful person is certainly desirable, but such beauty should point us to higher beauties. At the top is a beauty that is "itself by itself with itself," a beauty that is "always one in form; and all the other beautiful things share in that."[10] It is "the Beautiful itself," which is "absolute, pure, unmixed, not polluted by human flesh."[11] It is the "divine Beauty."[12] Surrounded by this beauty we who are pregnant with virtue, who desire to give birth to a higher way of life, give birth to the real thing, a truly virtuous and beautiful life:

> [I]n that life alone, when he looks at Beauty in the only way that Beauty can be seen—only then will it become possible for him to give birth not to images of virtue . . . but to true virtue (because he is in touch with the true Beauty). The love of the gods belongs to anyone who has given birth to true virtue and nourished it, and if any human being could become immortal, it would be he.[13]

The writings of Christian mystics have been full of a Christianized version of Diotima's Ladder, a process of ascent, a series of stages before the contemplative arrives at the unitive state.

10. Plato, *Symposium* 211b.
11. Plato, *Symposium* 211e.
12. Plato, *Symposium* 212a.
13. Plato, *Symposium* 212a.

Asceticism

There is no denying Plato tended to denigrate the body, even calling it a prison house for the soul. However, it is arguably only an age like ours that so completely obsesses over our bodies and over material things that could find Plato quite as reprehensible as we do. Plato's Socrates held that the practice of philosophy is a preparation for death. Death is the point at which we will enter a disembodied, pure state in which the good, the true, the beautiful will be crystal clear. For now, it is obscured by our bodily appetites and the way these keep making us attend to this world. Yet, in this world to which we become so inordinately attached, things are always either becoming or ceasing to be but never fully are. Nothing satisfies, nothing delivers on what it promises, and nothing lasts. Related to this, Socrates has a theory about what ghosts are. He says they are the disembodied spirits of people who have led their whole lives so attached to the transient things of this world as to never manage a complete break with the world of the seen, even at death. Their souls depart still "full of body."[14] They remain both visible and earth-bound, always hanging around graves and looking for bodies to inhabit. Philosophy guards against such an outcome by training the thinking person to become less attached to earthly things. Wisdom is thus "a kind of cleansing or purification."[15]

Here is an especially vivid moment in *Phaedo*:

> [E]very pleasure or pain provides, as it were, another nail to rivet the soul to the body and to weld them together. It makes the soul corporeal, so that it believes that truth is what the body says it is.[16]

A later stage of Platonism, which really began with the philosopher Plotinus (AD 205–270), went even further with the denial of the body. The "Neoplatonism" that Plotinus founded insisted that there must be a turning away from the world, all earthly things,

14. Plato, *Phaedo* 83d.
15. Plato, *Phaedo* 69c.
16. Plato, *Phaedo* 83d.

and the body, before the mystical journey can begin. It was this branch of Platonism that became formative of Augustine, and then of Pseudo-Dionysius and the whole Western mystical tradition.

NEOPLATONISM AND AUGUSTINE (AD 354–430)

Augustine of Hippo's importance to Christian theology and to Western thought in general is difficult to exaggerate and plenty has been written of him.[17] Here we are interested in the role of Neoplatonic thought in his spiritual life. He freely admits to reading the "books of the Platonists" in Book VII of his *Confessions.* His interest in Neoplatonism flourished at around the same time as his famous conversion in AD 386, which is described in Book VII of *Confessions.*[18]

One of the features of Plotinian thought that left an enduring mark on Augustine's theology was his belief in the importance of the inner self. Augustine is indebted to Plotinus as the philosopher that "presents the first powerful account of an inner world."[19] Augustine's move, according to Philip Cary, is simply to make Plotinus's *shared* inner world made of the faces, as it were, of all of us turned inwards towards the divine Mind into an *individual* inner world. He has to make this move because to fail to make it would be to affirm Plotinus's belief that this shared inward turn is possible because of a shared divinity that all souls have. Augustine's doctrine of creation *ex nihilo*, that is, that the created order did not simply emanate from the divine being but was made from nothing and continues to be distinct from him, does not allow this. Creation *ex nihilo* is an especially noteworthy correction of Plotinus. The inward turn is still necessary in Augustine's reckoning because of the need, already identified in Plotinus, to turn away from the allurements of the world, but, after this inward turn, there must

17. If you are completely new to him, Jonathan Hill's *History of Christian Thought*, 75–88, is a very interesting and accessible introduction.

18. Augustine, *Confessions* VII.9.

19. Cary, "Mythic Reality of the Autonomous Individual," 123.

be an *upward* gaze at the light of the Creator who is above us all. Augustine describes God's light shining over him:

> Under your [God's] guidance I entered into the depths of my soul, and this I was able to do because your aid befriended me. I entered, and with the eye of my soul, such as it was, I saw the Light that never changes casting its rays over the same eye of my soul, over my mind.[20]

PSEUDO-DIONYSIUS

Almost nothing certain is known about Pseudo-Dionysius but one thing that is widely agreed upon is that he is a "pseudo." He uses as a pseudonym the name of the convert of Paul's Mars Hill sermon, Dionysius, who is mentioned, alongside a woman called Damaris, as becoming a believer (Acts 17:34). The writings of Pseudo-Dionysius have been dated to the fifth or sixth century. However, pseudonymity cannot be allowed to overshadow the power of his writings, whose influence upon Western mysticism has been immense. Besides coining the term *monk*, he is also the inventor of the word *hierarchy*.

In dialogue with Plotinus, Pseudo-Dionysius insisted that to be solitary before the One entailed a stripping away, an aloneness that, according to Kevin Corrigan, "signifies primarily that which is without barriers or distinctions which could prevent the most complete union."[21] But it is also an encounter with that which is beyond words and beyond all perception since, by definition, the things that can be perceived and described are precisely the earthly things which need to be turned away from. The Divine is the opposite of all that:

> [L]eave behind you everything perceived and understood, everything perceptible and understandable, all that is not and all that is, and, with your understanding

20. Augustine, *Confessions* VII.10.

21. Corrigan, "Mysticism in Plotinus, Proclus, Gregory of Nyssa, and Pseudo-Dionysius," 42.

> laid aside, to strive upward as much as you can toward union with him who is beyond all being and knowledge. By an undivided and absolute abandonment of yourself and everything, shedding all and freed from all, you will be uplifted to the ray of the divine shadow which is above everything that is.[22]

The path to this union is the path of the ascetic who passes through purification and illumination before entering union.

BERNARD OF CLAIRVAUX (1090–1153)[23]

Moving now well into the twelfth century, there arose a new monastic movement that amounted to more than just a reform. It was centered at the Benedictine Abbey of Citeaux in the east of France, near Dijon. Historians sometimes call this period the twelfth-century renaissance. There was a flowering of art and literature. It was the age of chivalry and courtly love. The Cistercians (the adjectival form of Citeaux) emphasized human dignity and worth. They soon developed into a monastic order in their own right.

The most famous of the Cistercians by far was Bernard of Clairvaux. Continuing the affective, emotional tendencies of the age, Bernard was even more open about his feelings than his contemporaries. His spirituality centered on the love of God.

> The reason for loving God is God himself; and the measure of love due to him is immeasurable love. He gave himself for us, unworthy wretches. Hence, if one seeks for God's claim upon our love, here is the chiefest: because he first loved us.[24]

The most celebrated piece of writing Bernard left behind was his *Sermons on the Song of Songs.* The entire collection of eighty-six sermons still did not make up a complete exposition of the biblical book by the time Bernard died in 1153. Perhaps because of

22. Pseudo-Dionysius, *Mystical Theology* I.1, in *Complete Works.*
23. Much of this section has been adapted from my *Old Rugged Cross.*
24. Bernard of Clairvaux, *Love Without Measure*, 16–17.

the immense amount of time and effort invested in this text, it is claimed to be "one of the most celebrated and sumptuous religious texts of the Middle Ages."[25]

The reason for Bernard's attraction to the Song of Songs as a vehicle for his most dear convictions is probably the central place that union with Christ takes in his theology.[26] He is fond of the idea of a spiritual marriage, a unitive state that is available even to the most sinful and not the exclusive preserve of a spiritual elite, implying perhaps that the stages of purgation and illumination might not be strictly necessary. First Corinthians 6:17, which speaks of being one spirit with Christ in a way that is juxtaposed with the one flesh principle of marital unions, seems to have been especially important to Bernard in his reflections on the Song of Songs. The passage is referred to no less than fifty-four times.[27]

The bride, usually representing the individual soul courting the gender-neutral "Word" as the lover, but sometimes also the church with the fully gendered Christ as the Lover,[28] is exhorted to dwell in the wounds of Christ by continually meditating upon them: "[S]he hears 'My dove in the clefts of the rock,' because all her affections are preoccupied with the wounds of Christ; she abides in them by constant meditation."[29] The cleft of the rock is a womblike, invincible place of safety and childlike abdication.

Throughout the work, Bernard sounds almost Protestant in his insistence on the absolute sufficiency of Christ's mercy[30] and merit[31] over against human meriting. It is likely that this sounds as

25. Harrison, "'Jesus Wept,'" 434.

26. Fassetta, "Christocentric and Nuptial Mysticism of Saint Bernard," 358.

27. Fassetta, "Christocentric and Nuptial Mysticism of Saint Bernard," 347. See also McGinn, "Love, Knowledge, and Mystical Union."

28. E.g., Bernard, *On the Song of Songs* 61.I.1. See also Fassetta, "Christocentric and Nuptial Mysticism of Saint Bernard," 356.

29. Bernard, *On the Song of Songs* 61.III.1. Also 62.IV.7: "What greater cure for the wounds of conscience and for purifying the mind's acuity than to persevere in meditation on the wounds of Christ?"

30. Combined with "mercies," this word occurs thirty-six times in Eales's translation.

31. Occurs eighty-four times.

Protestant as it does simply because Martin Luther was himself so indebted to Bernard in his thoughts about the cross. In this place of trusting identification with the sufficient sacrifice of Christ, the merit of Christ's sacrifice can be shared by the "dove." Bernard writes:

> My merit therefore is the mercy of the Lord. Surely I am not devoid of merit as long as he is not of mercy . . . A righteousness that is ample and everlasting will amply cover both you and me. In me indeed it covers a multitude of sins . . . These are stored up for me in the clefts of the rock.[32]

TERESA OF AVILA (1515–1582)

The Discalced (or bare-footed) Carmelites, of which Teresa of Avila was the founder, represented one of many monastic reforms that took place during the Catholic Reformation. Teresa of Avila, also known as Teresa of Jesus, espoused a theology of the cross that has been likened to Martin Luther's,[33] with a personality that could also be matched to Luther's in that it was "individuated, passionate, uncompromising, indomitable."[34]

Teresa's spiritual breakthrough appears to have been stimulated by an *Ecce Homo* painting.[35] She remained resolutely devoted to the earthly, human Christ all her life. The cross was central even in her highest raptures of spiritual ecstasy.

Teresa's *Interior Castle*[36] is required reading to this day for anyone wanting to enter the Jesuits and has an enduring ability to resonate with readers' spiritual experiences. In this work she shows her indebtedness to Pseudo-Dionysius and the Neoplatonic

32. Bernard, *On the Song of Songs* 61.II.5.

33. Nugent, "What has Wittenberg to do with Avila?," 650.

34. Nugent, "What has Wittenberg to do with Avila?," 651.

35. Nugent, "What has Wittenberg to do with Avila?," 651.

36. Freely available online. See, for example, St. Teresa of Avila: *Interior Castle* or *The Mansions*—Christian Classics Ethereal Library.

journey within. It is assumed that the place to go to encounter God is within the human heart.

Teresa describes a crystal castle containing as many as a million rooms or dwellings (sometimes mistranslated as "mansions"). There are seven levels, named confusingly as both singular and plural at the same time: the first rooms, the second rooms, and so on. The seven sets of rooms correspond to the three stages of the mystical pathway: purgation, illumination, and union. The first to the third rooms are all part of the purgation stage. For example, on entering the first rooms, "His purity shows our foulness, and by meditating on His humility we find how very far we are from being humble."[37] A battle with self and with the devil ensues, leading to a dry period in the third rooms. We must push through, she says, "persevering in this poverty and detachment of soul,"[38] submitting our wills to the will of God.[39]

A big shift happens in the transition to the fourth and fifth rooms. Entering the fourth rooms may be difficult but finding it brings a new level. We become capable of the "prayer of quiet."[40] Distractions will come but there is now more ability to remain detached from the things of the world and quietly rest our souls in God. Entering the fifth rooms is the point of betrothal to Christ. We feel great love for the Lord and begin to express it to others. Our will no longer resists his will at all. In the sixth rooms betrothal takes place. In this place, we start to experience raptures. Teresa thinks we might even physically levitate. She herself had an experience of an ecstasy that was, at the same time, so painful that it was like the repeated stab of an arrow—a moment immortalized in the famous marble sculpture in St. Peter's Basilica in Rome. "The soul is now determined to take no other Bridegroom than our Lord," she says, "but He disregards its desires for its speedy espousals, wishing that these longings should become still more

37. Teresa, *Interior Castle* II.10.

38. Teresa, *Interior Castle* III.1.13.

39. Teresa, *Interior Castle* III.2.8.

40. Teresa, *Interior Castle* IV.1.2.

vehement and that this good, which far excels all other benefits, should be purchased at some cost to itself."[41]

Then, there is a painful passage between the sixth and seventh rooms in which one feels wholly unworthy, but this passage will lead to the marriage itself between the soul and the Lord, the seventh rooms. There, we enter a steady state of complete self-forgetfulness and unshakable joy. There is a clear understanding of one's union with the Trinity and all that this entails. "So mysterious is the secret," Teresa explains, "and so sublime the favour that God thus bestows instantaneously on the soul, that it feels a supreme delight, only to be described by saying that our Lord vouchsafes for the moment to reveal to it His own heavenly glory in a far more subtle way than by any vision or spiritual delight. As far as can be understood, I mean the spirit of this soul, is made one with God."[42]

So, as with Symeon, the rapture and delight of the unitive state is an experience that is available and to be celebrated. But for Teresa it only comes at the end of a lengthy process, which involves fasting, wearing hair shirts, and the decidedly un-Epicurean attitude of welcoming suffering. She was suspicious of her own visions and raptures and seems to have preferred not to have them because of how easy it is to be led astray by them. She regularly shared her experiences with those she respected, seeking spiritual wisdom and discernment. What is absent is the Orthodox emphasis on the prior union of the divine with the human in the incarnation. That characteristically Orthodox incarnational basis for the unitive state is not anywhere near as significant a feature of the mystical theology of either Bernard or Teresa.[43]

THE FRENCH QUIETISTS

The French Quietist tradition of the seventeenth century seems to have advocated a shorter path to the unitive state than Teresa's.

41. Teresa, *Interior Castle*, VI.1.2.

42. Teresa, *Interior Castle*, VII.2.3.

43. Stronger traces, though, can be found in Julian of Norwich. See my *Old Rugged Cross*, 68–72.

Leading figures were Francois Fenelon (1651–1715) and Madam Guyon (1648–1717). The Carmelite monk Brother Lawrence of the Resurrection (Birth name: Nicolas Herman, 1641–91) is often grouped together with them but was really a unique figure. He seems to have arrived at a perpetual awareness of his closeness to God not through purgations or visions, but just by dint of sheer determination to keep turning his heart towards a God whose presence he firmly believed was already there, even in the hustle and bustle of the monastery kitchen sink.

Here his biographer tells us about what Lawrence would do if the presence of God seemed to withdraw:

> [B]y a lifting of the heart, or by a sweet and loving gaze or by some words which love discovers in these encounters—as for example: "My God, here I am, all yours"; "Lord, fashion me according to thy heart." And then it appears to him that he experiences indeed that the God of love, satisfied with these few words, returns to rest and to repose in the very centre of his soul. The consciousness of these things makes him so aware that God is ever in the depths of his being, that he can conceive no doubt about it, whatever he does and whatever happens to him.[44]

Elsewhere Lawrence makes the astonishing claim: "I see him in a way which could at times make me say: 'I no longer believe, but see.' I experience what faith teaches us, and upon this assurance and practice of faith I shall live and die with him."[45]

The French mystical tradition largely did away with the self-mortifications of the older mystical traditions, its main selling point being that anyone could follow the path. Madam Guyon's techniques centered on the Prayer of Simple Regard, which was combined with an insistence (everywhere present in Guyon's *Experiencing the Depths of Jesus Christ*) that one need only look within to find Christ. Guyon eliminated the purgation stage[46] and did not

44. Lawrence, *Practice of the Presence of God*, 35–36.

45. Lawrence, *Practice of the Presence of God*, 55.

46. Though Lee seems to see a great deal of self-denial and mortification

seem to anticipate illuminations and visions. Guyon's approach proved highly influential on some strands within evangelicalism: the Moravians and their quietist doctrine (via her influence on Zinzendorf himself[47]), and the teachings of the early Keswick convention about "holiness by faith in Jesus and not by effort of my own."[48]

Guyon's founding moment of discovery is related in Upham's biography, which we'll be looking at in the next chapter. She reaches a point where she exclaims, in Augustinian-sounding words:

> Oh, my Lord! Thou wast in my heart, and demanded only the turning of my mind inward, to make me feel thy presence. Oh, infinite Goodness! Thou wast so near, and yet I ran hither and thither seeking thee, and yet found thee not. My life was a burden to me, and my happiness was within myself. I was poor in the midst of riches, and ready to perish with hunger near a table plentifully spread and a continual feast. Oh Beauty, ancient and new! Why have I known thee so late?[49]

In *Experiencing the Depths of Jesus Christ*, Guyon's aim is to provide a spiritual pathway that *anyone* can follow. It is designed for those who see themselves as not being any good at prayer. There are two preliminary stages, which both interact with each other: "Praying the Scripture," which is an abbreviated *Lectio Divina* in which an effort is made to internalize a portion of Scripture with a view to experiencing the presence of the Lord, and "Beholding the Lord," which seems to be a remedial step to take when the mind starts to wander. Scripture is again used to bring the mind back into focus and become quiet and still before the Lord. She also

---

woven into Guyon's method: see Lee, "Madam Jeanne Guyon," in Holder, ed., *Christian Spirituality*, 257–68.

47. Hindmarsh, *Evangelical Conversion Narrative*, 175.

48. Through Thomas Upham's highly popular *Life, Religious Opinions and Experience of Madam de la Mothe Guyon*.

49. Upham, *Life, Religious Opinions and Experience of Madam de la Mothe Guyon*, 13.

recommends, once quiet and stillness has been achieved, that we begin a slow, ponderous, line-by-line use of the Lord's Prayer.

There is then a further step, which she describes as the "Prayer of Simplicity," which describes the happy state of having arrived at undivided contemplation of the Lord.

> Perhaps you will begin to enjoy a sense of the Lord's presence. If that is the case, do not try to think of anything. Do not try to say anything. Do not try to do anything! As long as the Lord's presence continues, just remain there. Remain before Him exactly as you are.[50]

CONCLUSION

The writings of the Catholic mystical tradition—of which we have offered here only the thinnest of samples, omitting vast treasures—are rich in insights for anyone today who seeks a pathway to true joy and happiness. That experiences are available of true rapture and unfathomable delight is made very clear. In Bernard the end result is that true love is found, a love we may repose in, a love that exists for its own delightful sake, and a love that we can hide in like the dove in the clefts of a rock. In Teresa, true peace and everlasting repose is found in which both the highs and the lows of the mystical journey are over and there is rest in Christ.

Despite recent moves toward a new kind of monasticism that does not rely on withdrawal from the world, much of the writings of the Christian mystics of both East and West are the product of the devout schedule of the monasteries. Most people, then as now, do not have this luxury. This is why Madam Guyon's appeal has been so strong. With her it becomes clear that the unitive state is as near as discovering Christ within us. All that is needed is to quieten ourselves enough to pay attention to the presence. Even in the midst of busyness, Brother Lawrence was able to pay attention by offering little clipped phrases of adoration and yieldedness to the Lord. After twenty years of such a practice, the presence of

50. Guyon, *Experiencing the Depths of Jesus Christ*, 22–23.

God in his life was so real it was as though faith itself was no longer needed.

Something that unites the mystics of both East and West is the conviction that the unitive state, or the state of deification, is an end in itself. In the holiness and higher life movements of evangelicalism, union with Christ was a resource increasingly drawn upon by those seeking the elusive breakthroughs of sanctification. It was of interest mainly as a means to this end. To these movements we now turn.

4.

Evangelical Holiness

JOHN WESLEY AND SANCTIFICATION

John Wesley's doctrine of sanctification was a source of much misunderstanding and controversy during his lifetime and has been distorted by well-meaning proponents and denounced by impassioned opponents hundreds of years after his death.[1] Put simply, the two big misunderstandings seem to have been that he was encouraging people to claim that they have attained to *sinless* perfection and, secondly, that he viewed them as having entered this state as a result of a sudden experience that zapped them at some point *after* their initial conversion. This second experience became known first as the "second blessing" and later as the "baptism in the Holy Spirit."

Wesleyan scholars the world over have continued to pore over Wesley's journals and sermons, and his brother's hymns, and have closely read all the many authors that Wesley read in an effort to get at what he actually meant and where his ideas came from. Probably the best way to gain a balanced understanding of Wesley's ideas is to place his doctrine of sanctification within his

1. The most vociferous opponent I'm thinking of is B. B. Warfield in his *Studies in Perfectionism,* originally published in 1958.

wider concept of the *ordo salutis* or order of salvation.[2] First there is *prevenient* or preceding grace. This is the grace that is at work within every person *before* they come to faith. Each person is so acted upon by this grace that they must actively resist it in order to remain an unbeliever. Once a person succumbs, they experience *justifying* grace by which they are instantly pardoned by pure faith. But there is a second part to this, which is that, simultaneously, a process of initial sanctification is started. This is the beginning of *sanctifying* grace. The person is, thus, born again. However, this is not "full salvation," and the believer, though certainly heaven-bound, may struggle for years with a yet incomplete victory over powerful sinful urges. But there comes a point when they are moved to look to God for a further work of sanctifying grace. As they seek God for this, there may come at some point a more radically transforming experience. It is a glorious transition moment within a lifelong process of sanctification, a sudden jolt forward. After this transition, the believer is on the path to entire sanctification: an entire removal of all sinful urges and their replacement by the urge to love God and neighbor continually. Wesley believed the full and final attainment of entire sanctification was, in principle, possible in this life. However, while, as we will see shortly, he could point to many examples of the decisive transition, he knew of no examples of that final completion, and never claimed it for himself.[3]

Wesley's *A Plain Account of Christian Perfection* has been described as a "veritable manifesto"[4] for all the holiness groups that would later come into being in the nineteenth century. It is without doubt, however, that the writing of this book, Wesley's most sustained treatment of a second work of grace, would not have taken place were it not for a series of events that together make up

2. Here, I am much indebted to the uncommon clarity, balance, and incisiveness of George Bailey's dissertation, "Growing into God."

3. Parts of what follows have been adapted from my *Old Rugged Cross*, 107–10.

4. "This eighty-one page document has served as a veritable manifesto for all the holiness and perfectionist groups that have separated from Methodism during the past two centuries." Synan, *Pentecostal-Holiness Tradition*, 6.

the Perfectionist Revival or Otley Revival of the 1760s. Of the year 1760, Wesley himself records:

> Here began that glorious work of sanctification which had been nearly at a stand for twenty years. From time to time it spread, first through parts of Yorkshire, afterward in London, then through most parts of England, next to Dublin, Limerick, and through the south and west of Ireland. And wherever the work of sanctification increased, the whole work of God increased in all its branches.[5]

A characteristic of this revival, which was clearly by no means restricted to the Yorkshire village of Otley, was that it affected "long-established believers."[6] The beginning point appears to have been a meeting held in Otley in February 1760,[7] but very soon Wesley was able to collect hundreds of personal testimonies of people who, following a struggle with a strong sense of sin and failure, came through to a point of liberty.[8]

One of these testimonies was noteworthy enough for Wesley to include it in his *Plain Account.* It is that of Jane Cooper, who heard Wesley speak on Galatians 5:5: "For we, through the Spirit, eagerly wait for the righteousness of faith." This awakened in her the desire to be "truly happy." She then spent much of the week seeking a deeper experience of Christ: "I was kept watching unto prayer, sometimes in much distress, at other times in patient expectation of the blessing." Finally, with the aid of someone praying with her, she got her breakthrough:

> I was in a moment enabled to lay hold on Jesus Christ. And found salvation by simple faith. He assured me the Lord, the King, was in the midst of me, and that I should see evil no more . . . I saw Jesus altogether lovely; and knew he was mine in all his offices. And, glory be to him, He now reigns my heart without a rival. I find no will but

5. Heitzenrater, ed., *Works of John Wesley* 9: *Methodist Societies*, 473–44.

6. Staniforth, *Methodist Pentecost*, 7.

7. Heitzenrater, ed., *Works of John Wesley* 9: *Methodist Societies*, 473.

8. These numbered around 400 by 1762: Staniforth, *Methodist Pentecost*, 12.

> his. I feel no pride; nor any affection but what is placed on Him. I know it is by faith I stand; and that watching unto prayer must be the guard of faith. I am happy in God this moment, and I believe for the next.[9]

HOLINESS AND HIGHER LIFE

Martin Luther, and the Protestant theology that he inspired, had insisted that only justification can be a once-only affair, instant and complete, while sanctification needed to be relegated to a long, slow process, never complete in this life. The reason was that, if sanctification was included at the beginning, it might creep back into the place it occupied within Roman Catholicism, as the thing that *brought about* our salvation: we sanctify ourselves with penances and sacraments, *and then* we are saved. This was out of the question for Luther. Subsequent generations of Protestants heartily agreed: entrance into salvation must be by grace through faith—but then what? Too many sincere believers were finding that the gradual process of sanctification was, in reality, a daily experience of defeat and failure and with few answers other than to keep on being forgiven.

By around 1830 American Methodism, though enjoying enormous success, had begun to neglect its own most treasured doctrine, that of Christian Perfection. Before long movements were afoot to revive the doctrine. Phoebe Palmer, and her sister Sarah Lankford, were the first to try to revive Wesleyan ideas about entire sanctification within American Methodism. They started the "Tuesday Meeting for the Promotion of Holiness" held at the Palmers' home, and the magazine, *Guide to Holiness*.[10] Interest in the second blessing seems to have spread very quickly and by the 1840s perfectionist ideas had even spread amongst the Presbyterians and Congregationalists. There was "a veritable flood of perfectionistic teaching."[11]

9. Heitzenrater, ed., *Works of John Wesley* 13: *Treatises* II, 183–84.
10. Synan, *Pentecostal-Holiness Tradition*, 18.
11. Synan, *Pentecostal-Holiness Tradition*, 17.

Once her own experience of sanctification was complete, Palmer appears to have drawn two lessons from it that would go on to dominate her preaching on the subject. Firstly, she came to understand the importance of testimony. She felt that her side of her covenant with the Lord would be that she would agree to tell others of her experience.[12] Failure to testify could lead to the loss of the benefits of the experience. Secondly, Palmer's own story taught her to value the experience of being cleansed by God as the Spirit applies the benefits of the blood of Christ. Her altar theology was a description of the pathway to entering fully into a cleansed state, because, citing Matthew 23:19, it's the altar that sanctifies the gift. The key was that, having totally surrendered our entire self upon the altar of God, we must keep it there and not take it back.

Her altar theology simplified Wesley's suggestive ideas about Christian perfection and made them into a system, a three-step process: consecration (laying your all upon the altar), faith (leaving it there and trusting God to sanctify the gift), and testimony (being willing to tell others that you have received your sanctification).[13] No feelings or other evidences were needed, only faith. It is an act of pure faith, faith in what is effectively already ours because of Christ's redemptive work.[14] And one may assume that the tangible effects will soon follow.

On the UK side of the Atlantic, the Keswick Convention came into being. It was birthed as a result of the visits of Robert and Hannah Pearsall Smith from America in September 1874 to a conference at Oxford, leading, in June 1875 to the first Keswick Convention for the Promotion of Practical Holiness. While emphases have shifted and evolved over time, the Keswick Convention, located in the beautiful Lake District national park in northern England, is still going strong. However, in the 1960s, two attacks upon its distinctive emphasis on sanctification came from respected evangelical figures. First J. I. Packer and then John Stott seem to have contributed to a marked decline in proclamation

12. White, *Beauty of Holiness*, 20–21.

13. White, *Beauty of Holiness*, 136.

14. Palmer, *Faith and its Effects*, 52ff.

from the platform of the distinctive experience of sanctification in Christ that had been at the heart of early Keswick.[15] Coupled with this was that the charismatic movement, also in the 1960s, somewhat outmaneuvered Keswick's historic emphasis on the importance of the Spirit-filled life. Today, even where Romans 6-related themes might still get an airing, these are no longer being taught by speakers who can claim their own transformative experience of holiness by faith in Jesus. All the early leaders of Keswick could claim to have had a distinct experience of entering into a "deeper" or "higher" Christian life. It was what they said that made Keswick such a profoundly influential movement, not only spawning many similar conventions in Wales, South Africa, Australia, and New Zealand, but also having a direct influence on missionaries such as Amy Carmichael, James Hudson Taylor, C. T. Studd, and Norman Grubb. Via its formative influence on Frank Buchman, it inspired the Oxford Movement, which in turn gave rise to Alcoholics Anonymous. The core ideas of the first three steps of all twelve-step recovery programs are pure Keswick. The Welsh Revival itself was caused directly by the Welsh version of Keswick, and Evan Roberts received his "Bend the Church, save the People" commissioning experience at a small Keswick-style convention for seeking the deeper life. The two Christian publishers, the UK-based IVP, together with its American cousin, and SCM, would not exist if it were not for student-focused initiatives started by Keswick. The speakers sympathetic to the movement and its message and who spoke at Keswick would necessarily start with Billy Graham, but after that would grow into a list of speakers so long it would take up too much space to write it. But my point has hopefully been made well enough. The message of Keswick—identification with

15. Bebbington holds that the Keswick or Higher Life version of sanctification not only became mainstream within evangelicalism but was the norm until at least the 1950s, though the expectation of a definite crisis experience was dropped quite early on. Bebbington, "Holiness in the Evangelical Tradition," 309. See also Price and Randall, *Transforming Keswick*, 221–227; 235–244, which highlights the impact of Packer and Stott.

Christ in his death and resurrection leading to a life of victory—has been, in its time, highly influential, but has now been all but forgotten.

A Keswick week (now consisting of more than one week) was structured to curate a transformative experience centered on union with Christ in his death, resurrection, and ascension:

Monday: Heart Searching. "Confession and renunciation of sin."

Tuesday: Consecration. "Recognition of Christ's claim, privilege of being wholly the Lord's. Consecration in relation to the Life of Holiness . . ."

Wednesday: Faith. "Faith in relation to triumph, progress, service, fruitfulness . . ."

Thursday: Fullness of the Holy Ghost. "Fulness of the Spirit in relation to the Will of God."[16]

The slogan at Keswick was "Holiness by faith in Jesus, not by effort of my own."[17] It was a holiness that was the life of Christ himself within the heart, and was brought about by a simple but profound surrender to, and continuing faith in, Christ's all-sufficiency.

This teaching was designed to fill a yawning spiritual discontent. The sentiments of William Boardman are typical: "Forgiveness did not satisfy me," he wrote in his landmark book. "I wanted the dominion of sin destroyed. Purification, not less than pardon, I saw to be required."[18] He came to be convinced of a "present Savior" who "does actually deliver the trusting soul from the cruel bondage of its chains under sin, now in this present time."[19]

It is William Boardman that gives to the earliest days of Keswick language somewhat evocative of Wesleyanism in that a

16. Price and Randall, *Transforming Keswick*, plate 4.

17. Aldis, *Message of Keswick and its Meaning*, 39. It is a line from a hymn by Frances Ridley Havergal, often sung at Keswick: "Holiness by faith in Jesus, Not by effort of thine own, Sin's dominion crushed and broken, By the power of grace alone; God's own holiness within Thee, His own beauty on Thy brow; This shall be thy pilgrim brightness, This thy blessèd portion now."

18. Boardman, *Higher Christian Life*, 140.

19. Boardman, *Higher Christian Life*, 266.

second stage, a "second conversion" is to be sought. This he described as a "deeper work of grace, a fuller apprehension of Christ, a more complete and abiding union with him than at the first."[20] It is "a higher height and a deeper depth."[21] He laments that it can often be harder to persuade oneself, let alone anyone else, to enter the second conversion than it was to enter the first conversion,[22] but, having done so, one can expect that "in the new light all things take on a new loveliness, and from the new starting point the race becomes swifter and yet easier."[23]

Hannah Whitall Smith (1832–1911)

Pennsylvania Quaker Hannah Whitall Smith and her husband played a formative part in the beginnings of Keswick theology. The basic structure of her system is not dissimilar to Palmer's: "To sum up then," she says, "in order to enter into this blessed interior life of rest and triumph, you have two steps to take,—first, entire abandonment; and second, absolute faith."[24]

She describes this entire abandonment, inviting the reader to pray:

> Here, Lord, I abandon myself to thee. I have tried in every way I could think of to manage myself, and to make myself what I know I ought to be, but have always failed. Now I give it up to thee. Do thou take entire possession of me.[25]

She counsels that a restful state is to be aimed at:

> Relax every strain, and lay off every burden. Let yourself go in a perfect abandonment of ease and comfort, sure that, since He holds you up, you are perfectly safe. Your

20. Boardman, *Higher Christian Life*, 48.
21. Boardman, *Higher Christian Life*, 19.
22. Boardman, *Higher Christian Life*, 55.
23. Boardman, *Higher Christian Life*, 23.
24. Whitall Smith, *Christian's Secret*, 54.
25. Whitall Smith, *Christian's Secret*, 39.

> part is simply to rest. His part is to sustain you; and He cannot fail.[26]

A recurring theme of Keswick teaching is anticipated by her: don't look for feelings. The aim was that something takes place within the will, the deep motivational center of our souls. She is fond of a saying attributed to Francois Fenelon, one of the French Quietists: "true religion resides in the will alone."[27] She echoes Madam Guyon, in desiring that our wills become one with the will of God.[28]

If this consecration, this absolute letting go, is accompanied by faith in the sufficiency of Christ and all that he has done, then such faith is sure to "unlock the whole treasure-house of God."[29]

For our purposes, the eudaimonic element is especially noteworthy. This pathway is the pathway to holiness and happiness; it is the Christian's secret of a happy life.

Jessie Penn-Lewis (1861–1927)

Jessie Penn-Lewis was the most celebrated female speaker at the convention, though she later grew frustrated with its diminishing openness to the ministry of women, and from 1910 launched out more on her own, editing the magazine *The Overcomer.* Her teachings were filled with a monolithic emphasis on the cross, making it clear that the work of Christ was not only for the sins of the believer but for the believer's very self: "Calvary means that Christ not only bore on that Tree your sins, but that He carried to the Tree the sinner—carried you there."[30] But how does this work? Penn-Lewis is not the first, or the last, to have seen that there is a relationship between the crucified state already accomplished and the cross yet to be carried.[31] There is an inseparable relationship in

26. Whitall Smith, *Christian's Secret*, 43.

27. Whitall Smith, *Christian's Secret*, 80, 82.

28. Whitall Smith, *Christian's Secret*, 87.

29. Whitall Smith, *Christian's Secret*, 42.

30. Penn-Lewis, *More Than Conquerors*, 3.

31. A brilliant academic treatment of this is Tannehill's *Dying and Rising with Christ.*

her mind between the done deal of Romans 6 and the command of Christ to take up our cross (she quotes from: Matthew 10:38; 16:24; Mark 8:34; Luke 9:23; 14:27):[32]

> [I]n the writings of Paul there is a union with Christ's death which admits us into a new sphere of life, whence we look back upon a gulf fixed between us and the past; and we have seen also a *continuous* conformity to the death of Christ, which is a necessary condition for the ever increasing manifestation of the power of the resurrection reality.[33]

She offers no spiritual practices by which we may take up the cross daily but rather wants us to be forearmed with an attitude of abdication and surrender whenever we are confronted with situations that are beyond our capacity to deal with.

> [T]he taking of the cross will without doubt lead him [that is, the believer] into places where he will learn that he has no resources in himself, and he will be compelled to "*renounce all that he hath*" as of no avail to meet the forces brought against him by the terrible foe.[34]

Penn-Lewis is especially interesting, then, because by centering her doctrine of sanctification on the cross she is able to move seamlessly between the cross as self-mortification—an idea normally unwelcome in cheery evangelical circles—and the cross as gracious action within us. There is effectively no difference between the self-surrender advocated by all Keswick speakers as the *precondition* to the higher Christian life, and the attitude of resignation necessary to the taking up one's cross in a life of *ongoing* self-denial. And the cross is the emblem that unites it all.

32. Penn-Lewis, *Cross of Calvary*, 90–97.

33. Penn-Lewis, *Cross of Calvary*, 96 (emphasis original).

34. Penn-Lewis, *Cross of Calvary*, 97 (emphasis original).

Watchman Nee (1903–1972)

Watchman Nee (birth name: Nee To-sheng) references, with approval, Andrew Murray,[35] Hudson Taylor,[36] Jessie Penn-Lewis,[37] Hannah Whitall Smith,[38] and H. W. Webb-Peploe,[39] as well as the Keswick Convention itself.[40] Having died in 1972 after spending the last twenty years of his life imprisoned for his faith in China, he is, second perhaps to Norman Grubb, the last well-known speaker to carry the baton of Keswick teachings on holiness. His two most important works are *The Life That Wins*, which is a transcript of talks he gave in 1935, and *The Normal Christian Life*,[41] which represents his most mature thought and is compiled from talks given in 1938 to 1939.

Like Hannah Whitall Smith, he teaches a two-stage process towards entering into a more victorious Christian life: yielding and believing. However, Nee seems to have a way of taking Keswick ideas to their logical conclusion. His teaching is winsomely simple but to arrive at that simplicity he irons out all the nuances. So, the preliminary stage to our being willing to fully yield ourselves is that we must so despair of ourselves that we look upon ourselves as "worthy of death because we are useless and hopeless." He goes on: "'I have been crucified with Christ means that God was disappointed in me and that I, like Paul, have despaired of myself too."[42] It was also a common subtlety among Keswick speakers that they would try to avoid the Wesleyan idea of the eradication of sin, much to the ire of Wesleyans at the time, such as Reader Harris.[43] At Keswick the idea of counteraction, of sin being sidelined or set

35. Nee, *Life That Wins*, 20
36. Nee, *Life That Wins*, 22; *Normal Christian Life*, 38.
37. Nee, *Life That Wins*, 43.
38. Nee, *Life That Wins*, 74.
39. Nee, *Life That Wins*, 87–88.
40. Nee, *Life That Wins*, 143.
41. Nee, *Normal Christian Life*.
42. Nee, *Life That Wins*, 51.
43. Price and Randall, *Transforming Keswick*, 49–50.

aside, was preferred over against eradication. Nee went as far as to affirm that "Victory is Christ; it has nothing to do with me. I am still able to sin; I have not changed at all."[44] To affirm, as part of a teaching about how to be free from the lingering control of post-conversion sin that, "I have not changed at all," lacks logical sense. This kind of teaching seems to require mental gymnastics: we reckon such-and-such to be the case and believe such-and-such to be so despite the evidence. The evidence is a lie; the Word is the truth. Despite these extremes, Nee is, at his best, a valuable part of evangelicalism's great legacy of higher life teaching and his writings have retained widespread appeal.

Norman Grubb (1895–1993)

Norman Grubb and his wife, Pauline, came into contact with Jessie Penn-Lewis's "cross teaching" while serving in the Congo in the early 1920s. The teaching they heard from her centered around the believer's identification with Christ in his death and resurrection in Galatians 2:20. This passage became extremely important to the Grubbs. Pauline's breakthrough came quickly but Norman's was slowed by his tendency to look within himself to see whether any change in his character was yet visible. It was only as he learned to fix his attention on Christ living in him that he entered into true happiness: "He in me is the all, the joy, power, wisdom, victory—all. I transfer my attention, my recognition, my affirmation from the human vessel to Him whom it contains."[45] In time the number of people who, under his influence, also came to know and experience the reality of Christ in them—whom he referred to as "knowers"—grew large enough to hold a house party in 1974, which then grew to several hundred meeting every year in a large tent.[46] Grubb's death in 1993 probably marked the last enthusiastic exponent of the higher Christian life.

44. Nee, *Life That Wins*, 98.
45. Grubb, *Once Caught, No Escape*, 86.
46. Winter, "Norman P. Grubb—History."

CONCLUSION

A useful thing for us to note about the various brands of holiness teaching is how little they differ as to, firstly, the essential nature of what they are teaching us to look for and, secondly, the method by which we should try to obtain it. As to the first thing, it is clear that to those who experienced this second blessing or "second conversion," what is received is not an "it" at all. It is not a theological item or program but Christ himself. Boardman shied away from defining the experience in any other way than to say that it was a "deeper work of grace, a fuller apprehension of Christ, a more complete and abiding union with him than at the first."[47]

There is the recognition that, in a great many conversions, Christ does not seem to have been made Lord and king of the heart. He does not reign there without a rival and, after the initial honeymoon period, persistent problems start to emerge. But Christ does not enter in more deeply merely as the answer to these problems. People who experience this fullness become entirely caught up with *who he is* rather than what he can do for them and, in many cases, problems with recurring sin persist, at least for now. But, even when failure comes, there is an easier, quicker, and happier recovery. Where these teachings seem to have got a bad name is when they profess to offer an instant remedy for sin. Such claims lead either to disappointment or to dishonesty. The use of the term *perfection* has not helped.

As to the means or method: Firstly, there is *desire*. The presence of persistent failure or dryness in the life of a mature Christian brings a growing conviction that there must be something more available. Something is deficient. Once this desire is awakened, there appears to be a need to have *faith* in what this thing is that is missing: a higher life, a deeper life, a closer walk, something more of Christ, the "crucified life," the "exchanged life," or "full salvation." The possibility must be presented to the struggling Christian, using whatever terminology seems to fit, or else they will not know where to look for an answer. They will not

47. Boardman, *Higher Christian Life*, 48.

know that there is an answer. When there is a response of faith to the possibility presented, this response is always described as an act of *consecration*, surrender, or abandonment. It is likened to the process of conversion: we heard the gospel, and we handed our lives over to Christ. It is interesting that the first three steps of the twelve-step program of Alcoholics Anonymous adopts ideas that were originally inspired by higher life teaching. The first three steps involve a recognition of how unmanageable the problem has become (step 1), a realization that only a power greater than us can restore us to sanity (step 2), and then the crucial moment in which we turn our lives over to the care of God (step 3). We let go and let God. Effectively, we give up the fight and aim instead for "victory through surrender."[48] Many have pointed out how there may not initially be any feelings. Hannah Whital Smith, several times, quotes Fenelon: "Pure religion resides in the will alone."[49] But once this whole-hearted surrender to God has happened, faith is again needed in being able to rest and repose in the God to whom we are thus surrendered. It is an act of the will to truly surrender the self. It is an act of faith to keep it surrendered. And there may be no feelings to support either of them.

But, at some point, there is an epiphany, an experience, an unforgettable moment in which the nearness and reality of Christ is seen in an unprecedented way and all desire is focused on him. Again, this resembles initial conversion but seems to be a dramatic intensification of it. There is a singularity about the affections of the heart, to quote Jane Cooper once again: "I saw Jesus altogether lovely; and knew he was mine in all his offices. And, glory be to him, He now reigns my heart without a rival. I find no will but his."[50] Although this new depth of union with Christ will be tested and will need continual nurturing, life is never the same again. It is more than a cognitive breakthrough, more than an illumination, more than a eureka moment. A change seems to actually

48. The title of E. Stanley Jones's book, *Victory Through Surrender*.

49. E.g., Whitall Smith, *Christian's Secret*, 80, 82.

50. Heitzenrater, ed., *Works of John Wesley* 13: *Treatises* II, 183–84.

take place. It is a rearrangement of the soul's furniture. Christ has moved further in.

5.

Bringing It Together

Good News in an Epicurean World

In this brief chapter, I'll bring together what we have done so far in looking at the modern West as an Epicurean world and in seeing a deeply participative angle on the gospel as the right gospel to preach in this context.

I first need to bring into conversation the three areas of Christian tradition we have just explored: Orthodox theosis, the Catholic unitive state, and evangelical holiness and higher life. These are rarely brought together, though there has been some interest in looking at how theosis in the Eastern fathers had a formative role in Wesley's doctrine of sanctification.[1] Yet it seems to me that in bringing together these things we are bringing together some of the very most luminous moments in the history of Christian reflection upon what the life of faith entails. In fact, if we consider the Eastern fathers as a category in their own right for now, we can see that we get the very best of the fathers too: I'm thinking especially of the theological riches that flowed out of the Alexandrian and Cappadocian traditions that we drew on in the first half of chapter 2. Added to this is the golden age of Orthodoxy—the Byzantine era of Maximus, Symeon, Gregory Palamas,

1. See Bailey, "Growing into God"; McCormick, "Theosis in Chrysostom and Wesley."

and the countless other luminaries of the period and their explorations of theosis. And we have celebrated some of the very best of the Catholic writers ranging from the early Middle Ages to the late Reformation. Then we have drawn from the greatest legacy evangelicalism has ever given to the wider church and world—it's teachings about holiness and higher life.

THE UNION IS THE MESSAGE

The first useful thing that appears when we overlay all three traditions nicely puts to bed the most contentious thing about all holiness teachings: what in Pentecostal theology is called separation and subsequence. In other words, there is the assertion that the second blessing, however conceived, is conceptually distinct and separable from conversion and usually subsequent to it in time. This certainly became the working assumption of the holiness movement. And it is this aspect of the teaching that is problematic because of the way it can create two classes of Christian: those merely converted and those who have had their entire sanctification, who have received "full salvation." There is a definite family resemblance, of course, to the difficulties that came to a head during the charismatic movement, which implicitly elevated those who had received their baptism in the Holy Spirit over those who had not.

The Orthodox do not do this with their doctrine of theosis. For them, partaking of the divine nature, being inwardly divinized, is completely fundamental to the *whole Christian life* and is actuated symbiotically as a product of the believer's spiritual practices assisted by grace and the sacraments. Granted, they lack a second blessing, but they also don't have a strong concept of initial conversion either. All is sacramentally framed: birthed in baptism and fed by the table. The Roman Catholic tradition does have the sacrament of confirmation and, though the mystics we looked at would generally have conceived of the unitive state as the result of a process, they would not have conceived of their salvation as arriving in installments. If union with Christ is fundamental to our message, then it belongs, *in all its fullness,* at the very start and all the way through to the end. We are not saved by faith and then sanctified by some other means, nor justified to get us started and then introduced to everything else later, nor forgiven first and then sanctified when we start to mess up, or saved through evangelism and nurtured through discipleship, or saved to get us heaven-bound but awaiting a second stage to get us holy and happy in this life. The whole package needs to be offered *as the gospel,* as the way to peace and true happiness.

Second works of grace, bringing a deeper or fuller experience, ought to be the remedial exception, not the rule. Doubtless, however, the reality will be that the majority of Christians who long for a happier and more fruitful life of faith have not been introduced to anything further. For them, this will be a decisively second work of grace. But this is due to a deficiency in preaching and teaching rather than a necessary *ordo salutis.*

THE UNION IS THE UNION

E. Stanley Jones, who would often cast his net wide to speak of fundamental laws of the universe and the like, identified self-surrender as the fundamental and basic law of the Christian faith. He helpfully placed self-surrender between the teachings of the modern West and East. The West hails self-actualization as the answer, the East (by which he meant Hinduism and Buddhism) reveres self-annihilation as the answer. But the self should be neither actualized nor destroyed, he rightly said. Whatever Paul meant by the self being crucified, or the body of sin being done away with, and whatever Jesus meant by taking up the cross and denying self, it cannot have meant the annihilation of the self since this is impossible. They meant the surrender of the self. Yet, Jones seems to stop there. Other authors see self-surrender as only the gateway to deeper union, not an end in itself. By way of correcting E. Stanley Jones, I would therefore want to assert that the union itself is fundamental. This is what qualifies as one of the fundamental laws of the universe, if anything does. To speak in the cosmic manner of

Jones, we can observe that life is all about fusions and fissions—the two most powerful reactions known to science. And the most powerful things that ever happen to us are fusions with others and fissions from others. Union is life; separation is death.

Looking at things another way, possibly all the holiness authors make too much of a fetish out of sanctification. Holiness is only one of a myriad of blessings that flow *from* being in Christ and Christ being in us. But the union is the union. This is, as the Orthodox clearly saw, the *goal of God*: union with humanity—even entailing a union that did not exist before the fall. There is nothing greater than the union: neither the surrender of self that leads to it nor the sanctification that we hope flows out of it.

The teaching of John 15 on the vine and the branches reinforces this. The language of abiding de-instrumentalizes Christ. He is not the means to some end. Union with him is the end and in embracing this, we de-instrumentalize Christ, ourselves, and others. It is the answer to a frenetically meritocratic world. We *abide* in him, and he *abides* in us. The Catholic mystics saw this. The unitive state is the rapturous destination of the mystical journey. There is nothing greater that life can offer. It is unimaginable to Teresa of Avila that the unitive state finally reached would be then seen as the means to the end of sanctification, or more effective mission, or anything else.

THE UNION IS AN EXPERIENCE

All three traditions are of one voice in placing experience right at the heart of this union. Despite necessary cautions about looking for feelings, it is never seen as a merely cerebral or ceremonial union. Partaking of the divine nature, in someone like Symeon the New Theologian, means that the divine attributes are visibly shining through us. And Wesley was so keen to find empirical evidence of an inward change that he cross-examined hundreds of people who were claiming the experience. If we are not noticeably different after entering the union, or after entering more deeply into it, then nothing has really happened at all. We have deceived ourselves. There ought to be a different look in our eyes, a new frankness in our speech, a new warmth and humor in our personality, a new patience and joy about our daily life.

WHAT'S NEXT

We have said enough about what the Christian tradition suggests to us as good news to the poor in spirit. It is time for a more inductive approach as we look at a series of four New Testament passages that I hope could serve as good candidates for a series of teaching sessions or sermons as we hold out the offer of what I'm calling the Lifted Life.[2]

These four sessions could work well as a four-session teaching unit on a church away-day or as one-off Sunday morning messages. I have used illustrations and anecdotes in them that are personal to me. You should feel free to substitute these with your own and make as much use as you want of the ideas that follow. I am aware that it is potentially quite presumptuous and vain of me to offer up my sermon and teaching outlines as somehow exemplary. There are doubtless many readers that are much better speakers than me. What I am seeking to do is bridge the gap that persists between the high ideas of a Christian book, usually written by an academic, and the realities of ministry. There are other books, of course, that are entirely about the realities of ministry, but these tend to be rather light on high ideas—and I happen to find high ideas interesting. This is why I wanted to write something that does both.

OPENING DEVOTIONS

A little like the early Keswick weeks, if this was a four-session teaching unit, I would begin all four sessions with a ten-minute meditation, an exercise in Christ-centered self-care. This worked well when I tried it out at morning prayers where I work.

2. A term which I hope magnifies the one who graciously does the lifting and is hopefully free of the elitism implicit in the term "higher life."

Christ Despised

Leader: Isa 53:3–4: *He was despised and rejected by men, a man of sorrows and acquainted with grief; and as one from whom men hide their faces he was despised, and we esteemed him not. Surely he has borne our griefs and carried our sorrows.*

Everything Christ underwent, he underwent it as us. He experienced us. He took up the full experience of our humanity and healed it.

ALL: When you were rejected, mocked and beaten, it was my pain you carried

Christ on the cross

Leader: Luke 23:46: *Then Jesus, calling out with a loud voice, said, "Father, into your hands I commit my spirit!"*

Our own tendencies to keep acting against our better judgment can render us powerless. With Christ powerless and pinned to the cross and numbered with this transgressor, I need to say with him, "Father into your hands I commit my spirit."

ALL: Father, in my powerlessness, I turn my life over to your care. Into your hands I commit my spirit.

Christ entombed

Leader: Rom 6:4: *We were buried with him.*

On Holy Saturday, in that tomb with Christ, everything has finally stopped. All the shouting and accusation has been stilled. All the pain is over. All the fears and ambitions of those who brought about the crucifixion are no longer of any concern. It is the Sabbath, and the Man of Sorrows is at rest.

ALL: With you in that tomb, I too was laid to rest and all my strivings cease.

Christ raised

Leader: Rom 6:4: *just as Christ was raised from the dead by the glory of the Father, we too might walk in newness of life.*

I have been raised with him and walk about and go about my business in a new way, with new desires, and new loves.

ALL: As you live your risen life in me, may I walk in newness of life today.

Christ seated

Leader: Eph 2:6: . . . *and raised us up with him and seated us with him in the heavenly places in Christ Jesus*

Having offered one sacrifice for sins forever, Christ sat down at the right hand of the Father. Because his work was done, he sat down. Above and beyond my own to-do list there is the doneness of Christ's work. Seated with him, I am above and not beneath my circumstances. I have an elevated view and can reign with him.

ALL: I am raised together with you and seated together with you, and I now reign in life through you.

6.

Session 1: John 1:14

The Foundations for a Lifted Life

THIS FIRST SESSION ATTEMPTS to clear the ground. A significant proportion of the teachings of Jesus seems to have consisted of disabusing people of mistaken things they had believed. It was about unlearning what they had understood. Most of the Sermon on the Mount is about setting people free from shallow understandings of what righteousness is. Most of his parables are about weaning people off an entirely apocalyptic understanding of the Day of the Lord and teaching instead about a kingdom that has been inaugurated but would not be consummated this side of a gradual process, like growing seeds or spreading leaven.

Here in this session, we attempt to tackle nominalism[1]—the belief that a word such as *humanity* is only a word and does not refer to a real entity. And we attempt to tackle individualism—the belief that each person is fundamentally solitary and not capable of real unions with other persons. In so doing we hope to open the way to reinstating the full power of Christ's union with all

1. This originated in the Middle Ages as a correction of certain mostly distorted aspects of Platonism. A good article about nominalism is Rodriguez-Pereyra, "Nominalism in Metaphysics." Also worth a read is Tyson's *Returning to Reality*.

humanity through incarnation and the full reality of our union with Christ.

What follows is developed from a sermon I preached, in fear and trembling, in front of some local dignitaries at a big Christmas celebration in December 2023. The introductory parts are unchanged but the rest I have adapted beyond all recognition so that it is now probably more suitable for an already Christian audience. Here it is.

Mr. Randall, Madam Mayor, Councilor Creamer, and everyone here to today, what an absolute joy it is for me to be speaking to you about a subject so close to my heart. Not that Christmas is particularly close to my heart, to be honest. I know there are some people who absolutely love it and genuinely wish it could be Christmas every day. In fact, there are some younger members of my own family who have downloaded apps—as far back as last September—which tell them how many days, hours, minutes, and even seconds there are still to go until Christmas Day finally dawns. I'm the person who would prefer an app that could tell me how many days there are still to endure of George Michael crooning that last Christmas he gave someone his heart, but that this year, he's learned his lesson; he's gonna give it to someone special. I want an app that will tell me how many hours there are still to get through of fitting into an already packed schedule, a Christmas "do" of some kind: not only several major and minor work-related do's but little Christmassy get-togethers associated with just about every recreational group or voluntary association I have ever been a part of. I want to know how many minutes there are still to get through of those bursts of hot dry air that welcome you into the doorways of crowded shops full of worn faces, and how many seconds there are still to go of writing out nice messages in cards and deciding whether this person gets the rosy-cheeked Santa, or the badly painted snowy village. Please, just give me an app that tells me when it's all over!

But there is one thing about Christmas that is close to my heart. Given my profession as a theology lecturer, one would hope of course that Jesus, God, and all that sort of thing would be close to my heart, but there is one passage that I go back to again and again, and not just when it's Christmas. That passage is in John's Gospel, chapter one, verse fourteen:

> And the Word became flesh and dwelt among us, and we have seen his glory, glory as of the only Son from the Father, full of grace and truth.

IT'S UNEXPECTED

God had been speaking *words* to Israel for centuries. God had sent them prophets. There was no lack of words, words that could guide the people onto the path of peace. The trouble was with human nature. Humans, it seems, even when God sends extraordinary miracles to accompany his words, tend not to listen. So, it was time for a final Word. Not just more words but *the* Word; the last Word on what God is like: "The Word became flesh." This would be the very embodiment of God, not just another prophetic message. And this was a big surprise.

For sure, the Jewish people were expecting a messiah to come. But they were looking for a savior who would deliver them from the Romans in some mighty military conquest. They wanted a Deliverer that would annihilate their enemies, a divinely appointed King who would flatten the Roman legions and call fire down on Caesar's armies. That's the kind of last word they were hoping for. Instead, what did they see? A humble, softly spoken carpenter who, when he spoke, uttered the most profound teachings ever heard, and who with a gentle touch could heal the sick and raise the dead, but then he would tie a towel around his waist and wash his disciples' feet. They weren't expecting that.

Those of you who are single have doubtless got an idea in your head of what Mr. or Mrs. Right will be like. If you're anything like I was, you'll have created an image that is basically a female or male version of yourself: a future husband or wife made in your own image. Or maybe it was just me. I was a member of Fusion 101, which was kind of like Tinder for Christians. On this dating site I eventually included a certain blonde girl on my buddy list.

To be honest it took awhile for me to even take that step of putting her on my list of potentials. She was a bit scary, terrifying even. She had run the London marathon three times, the Great North Run twice, completed the three-peak challenge, plus a few triathlons here and there. She had traveled the world on various trips that took her to Southeast Asia, Southern Africa, South America, North America, Australia, New Zealand, and most of Europe. She had lived in Romania for a year, serving in an orphanage, and was a postgraduate-qualified pediatric renal dietitian. And she had a nice house in a nice village near Nottingham. I, however, lived in a rented bachelor pad on a busy street in a rundown part of Aldershot, and I walked each day to a desk job that was going nowhere and was poorly paid. The only impressive thing about me was that I was in the middle of an MA in theology, which I was doing in my spare time. After a glass or two of red wine, I finally plucked up the courage to message her. Immediately there was something that felt right. Very soon, I just knew she was the one. And here she is today, with our three kids staring at their Christmas Day countdown apps.

Because when God moves, it's always unexpected. When God acts, we say, "I wasn't expecting that." There is something very predictable about Christmas, which I think is part of the reason why I'm not its biggest fan. But there will always be something wonderfully unexpected about the Christ who gives Christmas its name.

In the words of crime novelist Dorothy L. Sayers:

> From the beginning of time until now it is only one thing which ever really happened . . . We may call this doctrine exhilarating or we may call it devastating, we may call it revelation or we may call it rubbish . . but if we call it dull then what in heaven's name is worthy to be called exciting?[2]

The incarnation of the Son of God is exciting because it really happened. However strange and extraordinary it may seem for God

2. Sayers, *Greatest Drama Ever Staged.*

Almighty to take on human flesh, God really did take that step down onto the dusty roads of Galilee, dwelling among us, walking among us, making this, as Tolkien observed, the one true myth to which all the other great myths were pointing. It involves God in an extraordinary self-emptying, a contraction, we might say. God appears as a helpless baby, showing a side to God's character that we don't normally associate with the supreme being. The word "became," in the Greek, is in the aorist tense, which signifies that there is no going back. It wasn't merely that he was born. It's that he permanently became something. God decided, it seems, to forever include humanity right at the center of his being. He permanently bound himself to us.

At the age of nineteen, in 1988, I wasn't consciously looking for him at all. I was a long-haired art student, a hippie stuck in the wrong decade. And I was into all the things that hippies are into. Although I wasn't looking for God, I had long been convinced that there had to be more to life. My comfortable middle-class upbringing had been quite stultifying at times. There had to be some other dimension, I thought. To cut a long story short, I found myself having very long conversations with a fellow art student about Jesus, mostly in the college bar. And every time we talked, I felt a presence I had never felt before. Someone other than me and my friend Dave was *there.* And often in the solitude of my room someone was there, someone glorious, someone whose radiance seemed to light up the grim surroundings of my student digs. An understanding slowly dawned over that summer, and I knew I had found what I had been dimly searching for. A light had entered my life that slowly became the light by which I saw everything else. Now everything made sense. Now there was hope. Before there was quiet desperation. Now there was a constant joy bubbling up that I had never experienced before. I wasn't expecting that.

He "dwelt among us." The Greek literally means that he pitched his tent among us, a deliberate echo of the way God dwelt in the midst of Israel when they wandered through the wilderness, led by Moses. Whenever Israel stopped, all the tribes of Israel pitched their tents around the big tent in the middle where the glory of God resided. John's Gospel is telling us that this has happened again in a new way, and not just for biblical Israel but for all humanity. God has pitched his tent right in the middle of the human race. The divine has entered humanity and dwelt there.

If this really did happen then something epoch-making took place on planet earth about two thousand years ago, in a smelly, fly-blown stable. But why would this be epoch-making? Why would this act of 2,000 years ago, however great it was, have anything to do with us today?

WHAT'S IT GOT TO DO WITH ME?

To explain the significance of this unexpected thing that has taken place in history, we need to clear the ground. When we hear the word *humanity* we think of it as nothing more than a word. It is one of those nonspecific, abstract words that tend not, in practice, to really mean much. We are more and more at home with specifics, less and less at home with big abstractions. Talk of "humanity" and we glaze over. Talk of the crisis in South Sudan and we are a little more interested. Talk of the antisocial behavior of teenagers setting off fireworks late at night just a few doors down from where we live, and we are even more interested. Specific humans are interesting, nonspecific humanity is not. And yet, almost everything Christians believe about Christ rests on the idea that *his* taking human flesh directly affects *all* human flesh. What he did in *that flesh* reverberates to *all flesh*. In other words, to be able to really get this—Christians included—we need to imagine a different way of thinking that most of us are used to.

The ancients seem to be better able than we are to think of humanity as really a thing, and of all humans as basically one entity. Humans, both living and departed, are all one. We are defined more by our oneness than by our individuality. The apostle Paul, for instance, was able to think of Adam, the biblically first human, as capable of representing all of us who share his human nature. In Paul's mind there most definitely is this wonderfully nonspecific thing called human nature that is genuinely shared and truly makes us all one, so much so that one human—Adam—represents us all. Even better, Paul was able to describe Christ in this way too:

> But the free gift is not like the trespass. For if many died through one man's trespass, much more have the grace of God and the free gift by the grace of that one man Jesus Christ abounded for many. (Rom 5:15)

Adam truly was part of us and stood in for us, but he messed up—like all of us would. But Jesus Christ came along and was every bit as human as Adam, and all the rest of us, yet did the right thing. He did not trespass but was supremely obedient. Because we are all one, the benefits of Christ's goodness as a human being can be shared by all of us. Somehow, it rubs off, it soaks in, it permeates us like medicine. They say, "all it takes is one bad apple," but Paul teaches that the effects of one supremely good apple can be even greater. Christ acts in a new way and renews us all.

We are accustomed to the daily litany of scandal and intrigue, peppered with all the usual "sex things, money things, and health things" that dominate our diet of news. We are accustomed to the way the news outlets keep trying to create the news by baying for blood so relentlessly that whoever is the latest scandalous person is forced to resign. And then we hope that someone new will take their place and that all the good that they do will permeate the entire organization or department they were responsible for. We entirely expect that to happen, so much so that we quickly move on to the next person whose head needs to roll. We assume a previously dysfunctional organization is now comprehensively fixed. Such cannot possibly be the case but such, according to Paul, is absolutely the case with the Second Adam. Christ has become the new head of Humanity Inc. and a new future has opened up.

In most Westernized cultures, we are highly individualistic. There is even a map available online[3] that can tell us which countries are the most individualistic and which ones are more collectivist. The more we think of ourselves as self-reliant and self-contained, the harder it is for us to think that the Son of God taking

3. Jiang, Wei, and Zhang, "Individualism vs. Collectivism."

on human nature could possibly have anything to do with us. We don't see that our shared human nature is genuinely porous to the influence of one part of it. Still less can we understand unions between specific humans. Even in a marriage, the once familiar Christian ideal of the two becoming one flesh is fading. Marriages today are more like a contract existing between two individuals, complete with prenuptial agreements about what happens if the contract is annulled. The Canadian philosopher Charles Taylor tells us that we have become "buffered selves." We see ourselves as having a kind of a force-field around us. There is a buffer zone that prevents us from truly merging any part of us with anything or anyone.

But let's have a look at what the Word becoming flesh might be. In other words, what is incarnation? What is divine enfleshment?

HE BECAME FLESH

Here is a marvelous quote from the Scottish theologian Donald Macleod:

> There is real change: change in the sense that in Christ God enters upon a whole new range of experiences and relationships. He experiences life . . . Before and apart from the incarnation, God knew such things by observation. But observation, even when it is that of omniscience, falls short of personal experience. That is what the incarnation made possible for God: real, personal experience of being human.[4]

God has always loved us and has always known us. He knows everything about us all. But there is a difference between knowing us by observation and knowing us by experience. The love of God is such that the Word *became* flesh. God, in Christ, *experienced* what it's like to be human. His love was so great he had to enter us! He experiences you. He experiences your trials, your fears. In taking on human nature, he was taking on specifically *your* human

4. Macleod, *Person of Christ*, 82.

nature. The shame he bore, the sorrows he endured, the griefs he carried were precisely and really *your* burdens that he made his own.

Paul says, "If one died for all then all died" (2 Cor 5:14). His death *really was* the death of all. He *was* us. He represented us because he was us. Christ made his own everything about us. Real renewal is possible because the Son of God has entered our nature and owned it, and then infused it with himself.

R. S. Franks put it this way, saying that because of Christ there is "a new ferment in human nature . . . renewing it to holiness and immortality."[5] To introduce a new, ordinary human into the great vat of humankind is one thing. But to introduce a *divine* human into the mix sets off a powerful fermentation process that won't have finished until the end of the age, when God gets to taste the mature wine. Thanks to the Word becoming flesh, divine renewal is underway, culminating in the resurrection from the dead. A new age has dawned. New possibilities are at hand. New dreams can be dreamed. New powers are within reach. Never before seen in-breakings of the kingdom can be expected.

> Long lay the world in sin and error pining,
> Till He appeared and the soul felt its worth.
> A thrill of hope, the weary world rejoices,
> For yonder breaks a new and glorious morn![6]

Isaiah says, "By his stripes we are healed" (Isa 53:5). The Hebrew word used here for healing refers to the act of sewing up a wound. So, there is a paradox: by means of one open wound another wound, my wound, is sewn up. It is because the Servant is human that he can be wounded at all, and because he became one with our humanity, his wound is the wound of all. The wounds of the many are in his wound. All your wounds are in his wound. But because the Servant is *divine* that same wound can become the *healing* wound for all of us. He is human because he is born of a

5. Franks, *Atonement*, 80–81.

6. Lyrics by Placide Cappeau (1808–77), translated by John S. Dwight (1813–93).

woman. He is the *healing* human because he is the divine human. The immortal God imparts immortality, the Holy One makes us partakers of the divine nature.

The heart and center of what was achieved was that God got personal with us and found a way, as one of us, to represent us and assume all that we are into himself. Out of that supreme act, lots of things cascade down to each one of us and can do so because of the unlimited nature of his divinity. Because of who he was that underwent what he underwent—not just as human but as divine—all is healed and all is redeemed. It was the *Word* that became flesh, and the *Word* that offered himself for us.

So, supposing we are convinced that this is for real, despite everything in our culture that screams at us that a historical individual's actions cannot directly affect us now, how might we experience the benefits of all this? How do we turn on the power? This leads me another area where we might need to imagine a different way of thinking about something.

BELIEVING IN HIS NAME

It's worth pointing out that John does not arrange things in order. We often need to look a few verses behind or ahead to get the complete picture. John does tell us what we are meant to do about the fact that the Word became flesh, but it comes a couple of verses earlier, interspersed with some stuff about John the Baptist. In verses 11 and 12 of chapter 1, he writes:

> He came to his own, and his own people did not receive him. But to all who did receive him, who believed in his name, he gave the right to become children of God.

That we would believe in Christ is the aim of the entire Gospel (John 21:25) and is the response he is looking for as we learn of God's only begotten Son having been given to us and for us (John 3:16). To all who will receive Christ, that is, to all who will believe in his name, there is given the right to become children of God. By faith, it seems, we enter a new kind of humanity, a begotten kind of humanity, a humanity that shares in Christ's own begottenness. We are no longer orphans but find that we belong to the Father just like the Son belongs to the Father and we find ourselves one with him just like the Son is one with the Father (John 14:18; 17:21, 23).

Clearly, then, this act of believing in his name is something more than believing something to be true. In today's culture, to have faith is to believe that something is the case, usually based on incomplete or contestable evidence. Faith is needed because we are almost sure but not quite. It's something not proven but accepted as probably true. But it differs not at all from other things that we believe to be true on more certain grounds. Being totally sure and almost sure are both alike a totally intellectual reality. We are not necessarily affected personally or changed in any way by something that we believe to be the case. The fact in question could have highly emotive or life-changing implications for us but in and of itself it is only a fact that has been believed to be the case. That's what we think faith is.

James says this: "You believe that there is one God. Good! Even the demons believe that—and shudder" (Jas 2:19). There's a huge difference, according to James, between "the Faith" and "faith." *The* Faith is what Christians agree to believe in whenever they say or sing the creed. It is a set of things that are believed to be the case. And the Jews had the Shema, "Hear O Israel the Lord our God is one God" (Deut 6:4). That's what James is referring to in the passage I just quoted. He had in mind people who thought that sort of believing was enough: they believed in one God and now they had also come to accept his Messiah, job done. But here, James would be on the same page as John in teaching that the kind of faith that really counts isn't the kind that simply believes that certain things are the case. True faith makes us into friends of God (Jas 2:23). Authentic faith is dynamic. In the Psalms, faith was all about making God into your refuge, your high tower, your fortress. Faith was about so trusting him, so leaning on him that he has become your house. He has become your dwelling place. You live there. You live in God. A French scholar once said, "There is a world of difference between learning to repeat 'God is an omnipotent being' and learning to address oneself straight to God saying, 'Thou art my Rock . . .'"[7]

In Psalm 3 the Psalmist is facing human judgment. People want to shame him for his faith: "O Lord, how many are my foes! Many are rising against me; many are saying of my soul, 'There is no salvation for him in God'" (Ps 3:1–2). But then, the psalmist declares: "But you, O Lord, are a shield about me, my glory, and the lifter of my head." By dwelling within God, he discovered that the shame being heaped upon him by people didn't matter. God was his glory. The threats and dangers didn't matter. God was his shield. It is this faith—the faith of ancient Israel—that the New Testament writers are assuming when they tell us to believe in Christ, or to believe in his name.

This then completes the picture: the Son of God, the Word, enters us by birth. We enter into the life of the Son of God by faith. And these two things combined have changed the lives of countless billions of people down the ages since the stable and the manger.

> The King of kings lay thus in lowly manger,
> In all our trials born to be our Friend.
> He knows our need—to our weakness is no stranger.
> Behold your King, before Him lowly bend![8]

CONCLUSION

That the Word became flesh means that flesh is a thing. It is a thing we all share. We have a common humanity, and the Son of God entered it. There was no exit from the human race once he had finished his earthly ministry. He remains embedded within this thing called humanity. The fact that humanity is indwelt now by God changes everything. There is now a "new ferment" released into the mix.

7. Regine Pernoud, in Radice, *Heloise and Abelard*, 35.

8. Lyrics by Placide Cappeau (1808–77), translated by John S. Dwight (1813–93).

I want to suggest that we are not buffered individuals but porous to the influence of those we are one with. Christ has entered truly into a union with you, taking you to the cross and bearing within himself all that you suffer. He is humanity-in-person and we can cement that union by joining ourselves to him in faith. We can enter into his life by putting our trust in him.

This kind of believing is not about knowing anything or being somehow sure of some contestable fact. It is about making Christ our dwelling place. It is about so leaning the weight of our lives upon him that we merge with him. We become stuck to him. We live in him and he lives in us. We make ourselves porous to his presence and, as I did when I was as an art student, we just might behold his glory.

7.

Session 2: Galatians 2:19–20

The Entrance to the Lifted Life

This session was given as a stand-alone sermon on October 27, 2024. Galatians 2:19–20 seems to work well for the times when we do not have the luxury of an extended amount of time with the people of God. I had just this one shot. It was delivered, within the space of forty minutes, to a lively, affluent Pentecostal congregation consisting of a very good range of ages and ethnic backgrounds. I was the guest speaker.

> For I, through the law, died to the law. I have been crucified with Christ. It is no longer I who live, but Christ who lives in me. And the life I now live in the flesh I live by faith in the Son of God, who loved me and gave himself for me.

INTRODUCTION: THE PENTHOUSE SUITE

I have often used a story that Louie Giglio once told. He had been invited to speak by a minister of a church who also owned a hotel. "You'll be thrilled!" the man assured Giglio. "I've given you the best room in the hotel." A church member came to pick Giglio up from the airport. "You're going to just love your room," the man oozed. "It's the best room in the hotel." As the hotel porter was showing Giglio to his room, he likewise said, "You've got the best room in the hotel." Giglio looked around at his room. It was okay but it was not *that* great. Later he went to the church to speak. The hotel owner, in attendance, asked, "So how do you like your room?" Giglio tried to be polite: "Yeah, it's good, it's fine." Not until the very last day of his stay did he notice a door that he had assumed was the door to the broom cupboard. He tried it. To his amazement, it opened out into a glorious suite the size of a large apartment, with a four-poster bed and panoramic views. The room he had been in was just a small adjoining room.[1]

The picture of the adjoining room is perfect. When we first believed we got the impression that we were about to be ushered into "the best room in the hotel." When, for whatever reason, the room does not live up to expectations—mainly because we discovered that we had not changed as much as we'd hoped—we just grow to accept it. We make ourselves at home in the adjoining room and get nice and religious. It begins to feel quite comfortable. What I'm about to introduce is nothing less than the way out of the adjoining room.

The longing for something more, even for those who have had spectacular conversions, is not new. It goes back at least as far as John Wesley. His whole Methodist movement was founded upon this very idea. Wesley was always promoting a second, deeper experience, describing it as full salvation, or entire sanctification. But not until quite late in life did he start to see examples of people entering into this second blessing. He interviewed Jane Cooper of Leeds, who had already been a Methodist for years but who, in 1761, suddenly developed an intense hunger for more of Jesus. She was intensely dissatisfied with the state of her soul. After a whole week of seeking him, she finally got it: "I saw Jesus altogether lovely . . . And, glory be to Him, He now reigns in my heart without a rival."[2] The early Keswick Convention, in the late nineteenth century, was also centered around a similar expectation.

1. Adapted from my *One with Christ*, 1. I am unsure about where I originally came across this story.

2. Quoted in Wesley, *Plain Account*, 64.

They called it the Higher Christian Life. Young mothers who had been at the end of their tether and shouting at the kids, would go along to a week of sessions in which they were taught how to enter into a crucified life and how to let Christ live in them, and how to restfully abide in him. They would go home utterly transformed. It was the Welsh version of Keswick that brought about the Welsh Revival of 1904. Frank Buchman experienced the Keswick Higher Life teaching and formed the Oxford Group, founded on the basic idea of surrendering your life, turning your life over to the care of God. This then became the inspiration for the twelve steps of Alcoholics Anonymous.

The Christians who became the very first Pentecostals were for the most part already steeped in either the Wesleyan or Keswick tradition and so already believed in some form of a sanctifying "second blessing." When the baptism of the Spirit came along, with tongues and other phenomena, this was a third blessing after sanctification. So, they now had three stages: conversion, sanctification in Christ, and baptism in the Spirit. Over time, that stage in the middle, that experience of the fullness of Christ, vanished, and, by the 1960s, all talk of being saved, *sanctified*, and baptized in the Holy Ghost had disappeared. Now we were just saved and baptized in the Holy Ghost. Watchman Nee, who died in 1972, would be one of the last well-known speakers that still taught the Keswick-style higher life idea.

I had rediscovered many of these teachers in the time just running up to my own experience of Christ in me in March 2024. I was enjoying Andrew Murray's *Abide in Christ* when, all of a sudden, on a very ordinary day, after having been a Christian for thirty-six years, it happened to me. I had been laboring over Paul's dying and rising-with and crucified-with passages for decades but now things were suddenly very clear, and I knew I was not the same anymore. I had had numerous blessed encounters with God, countless experiences of the Spirit and many moments of illumination, even revelation, but this was different. It was like a second conversion. I knew that everything had shifted. And, like my first conversion, though there was a honeymoon period lasting a couple of months of wave upon wave of intense emotion, it has now settled down into a daily reality. It has not all been plain sailing, but I remember something I said to my wife when I was trying to explain what happened. I said, "It's like he's just right there. All the time, he's right there!" And this has been the one constant. Whatever pressures I face both within and without, he's there in a way that's much more real than before. It's all so jaw-droppingly real. All these things that Paul speaks of can be experienced as real.

Not long after my experience I came across someone else who had also had the same experience. I was at the annual Cliff Festival, which is a Christian event hosted by the college where I work. I was giving a seminar about John Wesley, and I recognized someone in the audience who was a recently graduated masters student. He looked really different. His whole demeanor had changed. He even seemed to hold his head higher. I thought, "I wonder if he's had what I've had." In the seminar he very openly shared that he had been giving some teaching in his church about being in Christ and Christ being in us when, all of a sudden, he experienced it for real! He shared with us that he had been battling thoughts of an intrusive kind for most of his life, dating back to something that had happened to him in the past. But they were all gone.

As Pentecostals, then, we are used to the idea of a second and fuller work of the Spirit following our conversion. Some people might get the full package all at once but most of us seek the experience of the baptism in the Holy Spirit as something that can happen at any time after we first come to faith. What I'm proposing is that there is often a second and deeper work of *Christ* that is available too. There's a work of the Spirit but also a work of Christ. The Spirit gives us power to minister to others but Christ in us gives us power over ourselves, and is probably meant to come first, before we are anointed by the Spirit to bless others. I wonder how many moral falls in public ministry could have been avoided if these great speakers had received the kind of experience that Paul describes in this passage.

But even for those of us who are not experiencing serious moral failure but just a persistent feeling of inertia and dissatisfaction—like Jane Cooper—I passionately believe that this deeper work of Christ in us is the way out of the adjoining room and into the penthouse suite.

Firstly, then . . .

1. "I THROUGH THE LAW DIED TO THE LAW."

This phrase describes what we might call "*hitting bottom*." Paul went on to describe some years later, in his letter to the Romans, his experience of living under the law:

> I was once alive apart from the law, but when the commandment came, sin came alive and I died. The very commandment that promised life proved to be death to me. For sin, seizing an opportunity through the commandment, deceived me and through it killed me. (Rom 7:9–11)

He now saw the whole way of life dominated by attempting to meet a set of religious expectations as of a piece with the whole way of life he called "flesh." Everyone, whether religious or irreligious, lives under the power of the untamed zoo of feelings and appetites that is the life of the flesh. It's just that, for him, discovering forces within him that tripped him up even though he truly wanted to obey God's laws, indeed, discovering that these forces are actually *ignited by* the very laws that were meant to correct them, was a source of particular torment. So great was the inner conflict that, in the end, there was total collapse. He died to the law, and that's when the life of Christ took over.

The world of addiction therapy is always very interested in this hitting-bottom moment. It is a crucial turning point and until that happens, addicts are deemed to be only "playing the recovery game," or "dry drunks." Alcoholics Anonymous has built this hitting-bottom experience into its whole approach. Its founder, William Griffith Wilson (1895–1971), after finding his business activities were continually hampered by his completely out-of-control drinking habits, got to a point where he was admitted to the hospital. His friend Ebby Thatcher, sitting beside his bed, told him in no uncertain terms: "Realize you are licked, admit it, and get willing to turn your life over to the care of God." But Wilson wasn't quite at the bottom yet. Finally, a year later, he was in the hospital for the fourth time. It was at that point that a remarkable encounter took place:

> My depression deepened unbearably and finally it seemed to me as though I were at the very bottom of the pit. I still gagged badly on the notion of a Power greater than myself, but finally, just for the moment, the last vestige of my proud obstinacy was crushed. All at once I found myself crying out, "If there is a God, let Him show Himself! I am ready to do anything, anything'" . . . Suddenly the room lit up with a great white light. I was caught up into an ecstasy which there are no words to describe. It seemed to me, in a mind's eye, that I was on a mountain and that a wind not of air but of spirit was blowing. Slowly the ecstasy subsided. I lay on the bed, but for a time I was in another world, a new world of consciousness. All about me and through me was a wonderful feeling of Presence, and I thought to myself, "So this is the God of the preachers!"[3]

To have died is to have hit bottom. Paul described it as death to the law but for us it is death to all our attempts at doing things our way. It is to despair of ourselves so much that we are broken and powerless, just like Christ pinned to the cross. We are like a criminal on the run, a fugitive. We have reached that moment when we have run out of options, and we must hand ourselves in to the authorities. We admit that we are licked and hand ourselves in to God.

Martin Luther put it starkly: "When God brings to life, he does so by killing; when he justifies, then he does so by accusing us; when he brings us into heaven, he does so by leading us to hell."[4]

3. Wilson, *Alcoholics Anonymous*, 64.

4. *Martin Luther's Werke* 18, 633. This is Section 24 of his *The Bondage of the Will* of 1525.

Are you ready to agree with the divine verdict on your efforts? Are you ready to admit that your efforts to fix yourself are not working? Do you despair of yourself with a holy despair? Are you like Isaiah before the face of him who, surrounded by seraphim crying out "holy, holy, holy, Lord God Almighty, the whole earth is full of your glory," said, "woe is me, woe is me, for I am undone" (Isa 6:1–5)?

If that is you, then you are ready for the remedy that Paul gives us.

2. "I HAVE BEEN CRUCIFIED WITH CHRIST."

What on earth can it mean to have been crucified with Christ? What Paul has in mind here is perhaps revealed by his very next mention of the cross. At the end of the verse, he describes the way Christ loved him and gave himself for him. In the Greek there is the idea of a handing over. Christ handed himself over, he gave himself up at the cross.

There is a moment—though there are thousands like it in films—when, in *Mission Impossible: Dead Reckoning Part One*, Ethan and Grace find themselves on a runaway train. In fact it's the Orient Express, but it's now dangling from a cliff. They are both dangling from whatever they can hold onto inside one of the carriages, which is seconds away from breaking free of its coupling. However, an even more immediate concern is the grand piano that is just about to come loose from the hooks that were holding it to the now vertical floor of the carriage. Grace is hanging on to something that puts her in the flight path of the piano when it does come loose. Ethan is desperate to persuade her to jump across to where he is, but she is too scared. "Grace," he pleads, "You have to let go . . . Do you trust me, or not? You gotta trust me. Come on, Grace. Give me your hand. You gotta jump. Don't look up. Look at me. Trust me. I won't let you fall. I promise." The camera cuts to the feeble-looking brass hook holding the piano in place, which looks like it would struggle to hold up a wet raincoat. And, sure enough, it is now bending and creaking very loudly. Ethan raises his voice to be heard above the creaking of the hook: "I won't let you fall!" Overcome by urgency, Ethan feels the need to become a lot more direct. "Jump, Grace! Jump! You gotta trust me! Jump! Please!" She jumps but only just in time. She is in mid-flight on her way to the arms of Ethan when the piano breaks free and brushes past her legs in slow motion as it falls and spectacularly smashes through the back of the carriage. A predictable but somehow memorable cinematic moment, I thought. It was even more memorable because some of it was filmed near to where I work, in the Peak District. A real runaway steam train was constructed and filmed running over a cliff and smashing to pieces at the bottom of a disused quarry, much to the fascination of all the locals.

Faith is an act of surrender that brings us into the arms of God. Business experts still recommend that companies try to make time in the schedule for team-building days. These typically involve trust-building exercises. Companies with high trust levels are apparently 300 percent better performing, whatever that means. And we probably all know the most famous trust exercise called the trust fall. In the trust fall, colleagues form a circle around one person in the middle, who closes his or her eyes and falls backward, fully expecting someone to catch them. Simple though that may seem, it's a perfect picture of what true faith looks like. In the West we tend to have a very cerebral view of faith. We think that faith is about believing a set of things to be the case. And so, when we come to trying to get free of the things that hold us, we go for a program or spiritual regimen of some kind that is typically about believing in a set of things we assert to be the case. But, according to Paul, true faith is not faith in an *it* at all. If we trust fall into the arms of an *it*—a program, a technique, a spiritual discipline—the highly likely result, in the end, will be a loud thud. Instead, we trust fall into a person, and that person is Christ himself. And in doing this we find ourselves in the same territory as his own self-surrender at the cross. With him in the Garden we say, "not as I will but your will be done" (Luke 22:42), and trust fall into him. With him on the cross we say, "into your hands I commit my spirit" (Luke

23:46) and discover that we have entered a space where God is our dwelling place, our house, our fortress, our high tower

Rudolf Bultmann described believing as "the surrender of all seeming security and every pretense, the willingness to live by the strength of the invisible and uncontrollable."[5]

The life of faith is not a leap in the dark, but it is a leap. It is a paradigm shift from self-reliance to God-reliance. And, even for those who already have faith, each new breakthrough in the life of faith is entered by the same means as at the very start: the leap across from where you are to where you need to be.

The main thing, then, that Paul has in mind here, by saying that he has been crucified with Christ, is the *manner* of the crucifixion of Christ. As we saw, the clue to this is in the phrase, "the Son of God who loved me and gave himself for me." Paul never ceased to be amazed that Christ would so willingly hand himself over to the most humiliating, to the most painful, to the slowest and most drawn-out method of execution that humanity has ever devised. Paul was captivated by this and saw it as the ultimate demonstration of love. Christ *handed himself over* at the cross. That's why Paul gloried in the cross and made Rome's direst sanction into his greatest boast.

As Paul uses the phrase "gave himself" he more than likely had in mind the Greek version of Isaiah 53, which predicts how the Servant will *hand over his soul* to death for the sins of many (Isaiah 53:12). It was an act of free self-surrender. And this describes, too, Paul's participation in that cross. He, having come to the end of his own attempts at keeping the law of God, had handed himself over. He had exchanged his own life for something better. He had lost his life to find it in Christ. To be crucified with Christ is to have despaired of ourselves and to have handed ourselves over to God.

Here's Bultmann again:

> Man is not free in his inner being; when he withdraws from the world and knows that he is placed in the presence of God, he discovers that what he wills is not matched by his ability to do it, and that there is a schism

5. Bultmann, *Theology of the New Testament II*, 75.

> of his personality into two "I"s, so that he can experience freedom only as a freedom from himself. He achieves it in the surrender of his old "I," but in such a way that Christ is a new "I" in him.[6]

3. "CHRIST LIVES IN ME."

This now brings us to the next part in our passage: "It is no longer I who live, but Christ who lives in me." The Greek word order suggests a translation that might be like: "I live, yet no longer I." In the "yet no longer I" he introduces the word "egō," meaning "I," from which we get the words "ego" and "egotistical." While Paul is not here intending a meaning *exactly* like our modern word "ego," there is significance in the fact that he uses the "I" word at all. In Greek it is normally possible to let the hearer know you are referring to yourself simply in the form the verb takes. The verb itself already implies the "I." The "egō" is there, despite being a rare word in Paul, because he wants to draw attention to his "I." He is saying that in the life that he now lives, the central "I" of what was his life, the captain of his ship that once did all the navigating, has been replaced.

Christ lives his life in me. He is alive in me, being himself through me. The famous missionary Norman Grubb went to see the Welsh Revival chronicler Jessie Penn-Lewis, whose teachings on Galatians 2:20 had awakened his interest. He describes the meeting in this way: "[A]s she talked, it was like a great light lit within me, bringing the inner awareness which has never left me since, of Christ living in me; and living in such a sense that it was not I doing the living, but He in me, in His Norman form."[7] Perhaps this encapsulates the life of the indwelling Christ. He lives in me in a Ben Pugh sort of way. He can bring out those aspects of the image of God that I was made to especially reflect. And he can live through you in a you sort of way, bringing out the true youness of

6. Bultmann, *Essays Philosophical and Theological*, 141.

7. Grubb, *Once Caught, No Escape*, 84.

you. As someone once said, "You are never so much your own than when you are most his."[8]

You will be amazed at the sheer familiarity with which Christ is happy to relate to you, his proud ownership of you despite your flaws, and his willingness to be a part of you, to live through you in a you sort of way, joining in with the things you enjoy doing. And even if you mess up, you're his problem now. You are entirely his. We have to take our eyes off ourselves and not bother any more with monitoring how well we're doing. For as long as Christ is the focus, there is peace. You belong to Christ, and your life is Christ.

I have seen Christ live his life through many unique people, but the most outstanding one is a white-haired Canadian missionary who was staying at the house where I lived at that time. He was part of a team that had come from the Fire School of Ministry that had started in Pensacola, Florida, in the wake of the revival there that had taken place in 1995. I must have been in my late twenties. He sat with me one morning at the dining table, chatting away. He had been a latecomer to faith and was amazed by what God had done in him in his senior years. He kept saying, "Oh Brother, my heart is so full." The more he spoke, the more I could sense the presence of God all over him and flowing from him to me. I have met others that carry the presence of God with them, but none like this man. He was glowing. I went to the bathroom and glanced in the mirror. I was glowing too. In fact, I looked about ten years younger. My whole facial appearance had changed. It was an unforgettable experience of Christ living in and through an ordinary human being, a man in his late sixties or early seventies. Sadly, the anti-aging effects of this encounter soon wore off, but the experience was unforgettable. "He is my form . . ." says Luther in his comments on this passage, "my perfection, adorning and beautifying my faith. We cannot conceive spiritually how closely Christ is united to us. Christ lives this life in me that I now live; he himself is this life that I now live. Therefore Christ and I are one in this respect."[9]

8. Jones, *Victory Through Surrender*, 42.

9. Luther, *Galatians*, 106.

It's still possible to mess up but when we do we are aware that we are joined to him, we are glued to Christ, as Paul says in 1 Corinthians 6:17—we are stuck to him. It's not the case, when we make a mistake, that we have therefore "strayed" and must now find our way back. It's not that we've fallen from him and must now try to climb back up. If that were the case the church would be full of people that have just never made the climb. Rather, *even when we fail*, we are already there at that place where Christ can restore us. We haven't got to get somewhere first. We're already there. Paul says in Ephesians 2:13, "[N]ow in Christ Jesus you who *once were* far off *have been brought near* by the blood of Christ."

CONCLUSION

So then, I through the law, died to the law, came to the end of myself, despaired of self. I have been crucified with Christ, I have handed myself over. And now, Christ lives in me, having become the new motivational center of my being. That's how to get out of the adjoining room and start living in the penthouse suite.

I can perhaps best summarize this passage in the words of Watchman Nee:

> Our crucifixion with Christ is a glorious historic fact. Our deliverance from sin is based, not on what we can do, nor even on what God is going to do for us, but on what He has already done for us in Christ. When that fact dawns upon us and we rest back upon it (Rom. 6:11), then we have found the secret of a holy life.[10]

Learn the secret of entire self-surrender to Christ, so that your life is no longer centered on Captain Ego trying to be heard, trying to assert itself, trying to compete, getting offended, getting frustrated, getting lustful, getting fed up, and perhaps even trying to be religious. Why not just exchange your emptiness for Christ's fullness? Why not simply hand over your anxiety and swap it for his deep peace? Rest back upon it. Give him charge of your faults and foibles, and wait for his joy to fill you.

10. Nee, *Sit, Walk, Stand*, 17.

8.

Session 3: Romans 6:7–11

A Holy Saturday Faith

THIS SESSION MIGHT WORK as the after-lunch session of a morning's teaching. It is slower and less demanding than the previous two sessions and allows the participants to more deeply inhabit the story of the dying and rising of Christ. Here we move from Good Friday to Holy Saturday. I have noticed a change in the atmosphere when I invite people into the stillness of the tomb:

> We were buried therefore with him by baptism into death, in order that, just as Christ was raised from the dead by the glory of the Father, we too might walk in newness of life. For if we have been united with him in a death like his, we shall certainly be united with him in a resurrection like his. We know that our old self was crucified with him in order that the body of sin might be brought to nothing, so that we would no longer be enslaved to sin. For one who has died has been set free from sin. Now if we have died with Christ, we believe that we will also live with him. We know that Christ, being raised from the dead, will never die again; death no longer has dominion over him. For the death he died he died to sin, once for all, but the life he lives he lives to God. So you also must consider yourselves dead to sin and alive to God in Christ Jesus. (Rom 6:7–11)

USE YOUR IMAGINATION

This passage tends to not make much sense until we realize Paul is assuming we still have this thing called an imagination. He's saying,

> Imagine you are in that tomb with Jesus. The fight is over; all past struggles are now irrelevant; every temptation, not applicable; every expectation, someone else's burden. It's *over.* Everything is still. It is the Sabbath and Christ's once tortured body rests on a bed of stone, perfectly still. The Man of Sorrows is now a man of rest. Time seems to have stopped. It is not a place of action. Literally nothing is happening here in this tomb. But it is also a place of anticipation. Sunday is coming and we know that we will be part of that too.

Next, having put us there in imagination, Paul will slowly get us to see that this is rather more than an imaginative flight of fancy. An act of the imagination becomes an act of faith. It is a faith powered by a real acquaintance with and participation in the entombment of Christ. All that is past is past. What things were gain have been counted loss (Phil 3:7). "Remember not the former things," proclaims Isaiah, "nor consider the things of old. Behold, I will do a new thing. Now it shall spring forth" (Isa 43:19). We are about to enter the life of the age to come, the power of the new creation. Old things have passed away.

But it is a state of limbo, a liminal state. Such states are a common Hollywood trope. The hero has got to the end of their rope. They are finished, or at least that's what the character thinks. We, the audience, know this cannot possibly be the end. We have seen it so many times that we immediately recognize the trope. We know it is an in-between state. The mostly fictitious take on P. T. Barnum in the *The Greatest Showman* has him down on his luck, having lost everything and in a state of emotional paralysis, until his diverse dance troop finds him and talks some sense back into him. An almost identical scene is presented by Mr. Moon in *Sing*. Like Barnum's circus, his theater is destroyed, by a flood instead of a fire. Like Barnum, Mr. Moon has found seclusion in which to sulk. His normally sunny personality is broken. But along come all the contestants of the talent show that wasn't to be and they rouse him back into action. But the tomb of Christ differs in that, instead of finding ourselves unable to move because of circumstances, we *choose* the stillness of the in-between moment. This state need not have been brought on by failure or an unforeseen reversal—though it may have been. But the point is we choose passivity. We make friends with our natural helplessness and choose to wait for the power of God. We do not act but wait to be acted upon.

Let's see if we can find out some more about what this might look like.

GET RESTED

Paul has much to say about employment. He says that our old self was crucified with Christ and that this rendered the sinful way of life literally unemployed (Rom 6:6). He talks about the wages of sin. He spends much time inviting us to picture ourselves as household servants who must present ourselves to the new master (Rom 6:13–23). To use a more contemporary image, Holy Saturday is about retirement, or perhaps a layoff and a severance package. The point is, we don't serve our old employer any more, and Holy Saturday is a space where we enjoy that fact. It is faithful passivity, a joyful serenity. It is what the mystics would call the dark night of the soul but perhaps a more cheerful version of it.

To simply stop is a hard thing in today's world. On the eve of the COVID-19 pandemic I had been getting so tired that I kept asking, "God, please make it stop." Suddenly, it seemed, he did. Suddenly, everything stopped—or went online. Some have even described the "Michelangelo effect." For many, far from the pandemic having been a negative experience, it was just what they needed. It gave them the space to discover, like Michelangelo chiseling away at a block of marble, what sort of shape they really were. They rediscovered themselves, with life-changing consequences. This is the power of stopping, the power of Sabbath. Hebrews

4:9–10 says, "So then, there remains a Sabbath rest for the people of God, for whoever has entered God's rest has also rested from his works as God did from his." To enter God's rest is to start upon your life's true work, but not until we have begun this way will there be a true beginning to anything.

The Holy Saturday experience is an experience of not needing to do anything. Postmortems are not needed. Breast-beating is not required. We just stay where we are because where we are is good. Meditative techniques can help us to stay put in a Holy Saturday faith. Many of the Orthodox monks were convinced that the best way to make union with Christ seem more real is to practice stillness. And being still certainly seems to be the best way to lean into this state. It does not require an elaborate technique: breathing through the Jesus Prayer will do, inhaling through "Lord, Jesus, Christ, Son, of God . . ." holding it and then slowly breathing out through "have, mercy on me." Or, a Polish colleague of mine tells of spending very long periods in meditation by focusing on nothing else than the idea of letting go, letting go of absolutely everything, especially things he cannot control. He just lets go. His life exudes calm.

GET FREE

"He who has died has been freed from sin" (Rom 6:7). This is one of those rare moments when Paul lets us know the general principles he's working with. It's just like 1 Corinthians 6:17: "He who is joined to the Lord is one spirit with him." In fact, the two seem to go together: he who is joined to the Lord is one spirit with him and therefore has died with him and is hence freed from sin.

He who has died has been freed. But how have we died? We have been joined to him who has died. And so, we are free. He who has died is not about to do anything except receive the same Spirit that raised Jesus from the dead. He who has died has been freed and just needs to know it.

What sort of freedom is this? People have different definitions of freedom but probably the closest to Paul would be Isaiah Berlin's idea of a negative freedom. Positive freedom is the opportunity and capacity to fulfill one's purpose, the freedom to just go ahead and do whatever you want. Paul would probably have reservations about that because he was already being misunderstood as teaching that people can be justified by faith and then live how they please, without the need for any moral guidance. What Paul seems instead to emphasize is negative freedom, freedom *from* slavery to sin. It's freedom *from* the dominion of sin that Paul says is the result of being dead with an entombed Messiah.

I am the not-always-proud owner of a black labrador called Charlie. Mostly, he is a good boy, but his one terrible weakness is his appetite. And it is not necessarily an appetite for good food. He is a scavenger and has always been attracted to certain discarded and, shall we say, pre-digested, items that he encounters while on a walk with me. Once he picks up the scent of something disgusting in the bushes he disappears and becomes entirely unresponsive to the most vehement cries from his owner. On one occasion he was gone for about half an hour until he was found by another dog owner. A jogger passed me and, picking up on the troubled look on my face as I scoured the horizon, said, "Are you looking for a black labrador? He's with that lady on the path up there." I knew what Charlie was after but had foolishly thought the item would have fully decomposed after all the months since I had last come this way with him. It was a rabbit carcass. Sadly, as I found to my cost, rabbit carcasses become more, not less, appealing with age. They become useful not only for chewing but also for rolling in so that he can carry this well-rotted flesh scent everywhere he goes. I have stopped being amazed by how incomparably revolting a labrador's habits can be. Give me a rat for a pet any day.

Charlie is a picture of the power of sin in our lives. Our relationship with the Lord is still there, of course, but we have wandered off. We have disappeared, perhaps for hours, days, months, or even years, in pursuit of something worthless, or even disgusting. The Lord waits patiently for us to return—or to be found by a kind stranger. Holy Saturday is a state of having died to these enticing but deadly things. They lie *in the past* in a life that had its struggles but is now *over*. We are now still, and we do not stir. We rest with the Lord. We are in a state of powerless freedom.

But I want to revisit Paul's phrase again: "He who has died has been freed from sin." The Greek word translated as "freed" is in fact the word for "justified." He who has died has been justified from sin. It probably has the sense here of being "no longer answerable to," as in a court of law where the accused has been acquitted and is free to go—no criminal record, no stain on their reputation, free. But I think Paul's choice of word here signals to us that, for him, there are not two distinct works of the cross: Christ's death *for* sin on our behalf and Christ's death *to* sin in union with us. It is all a seamless garment. We are invited in this place of Holy Saturday rest to reflect again on Christ's sacrifice *for* sin. The writer to the Hebrews enthuses that through "one sacrifice for sins forever" (Heb 10:12), Christ made a final and complete atonement for sin and has sat down. His work is done. He rests, and so do we. The offering to end all offerings means that we can be freed from guilt.

Our levels of sin consciousness—both of past and present misdemeanors—will typically become more intense, not less intense, within a few weeks of entering the fullness of life in Christ. It is then that we become aware that we are carrying a load of guilt. But what is guilt? Paul Tournier said this: "It is inscribed in the human heart: everything must be paid for!"[1] Guilt leads to a kind of self-quantifying. We calculate that we owe something. We become aware that we cannot pay what we owe, and that sense of indebtedness affects our self-worth. We persistently feel that we are not enough. It's like having imposter syndrome but an imposter syndrome that spreads to every sphere of life. We are insufficient and not enough because we owe a debt we cannot pay. We feel inferior to others, even if we are the best qualified or most decorated person in the room.

The writer to the Hebrews surmises that if an offering could have been made that would finally take away sins, then the worshippers would have had "no more consciousness of sins" (Heb 10:2). He then goes on to spell out that this is exactly what has

1. Tournier, *Guilt and Grace*, 175–6.

happened. There has been an offering for sin that "perfects" or makes complete forever those who come to God through Christ (Heb 10:1,14). If we are complete, then it's because nothing is owed. And the offering was made long before you or I came into the world, long before we had done anything good or bad. The finality of the offering means that we can enjoy life in a permanent state of having "no more consciousness of sins" (Heb 10:2). We do not owe anything anymore and can rest in faith on the sufficiency of the atonement.

> Not all the blood of beasts
> on Jewish altars slain
> could give the guilty conscience peace
> or wash away the stain.
>
> But Christ, the heav'nly Lamb,
> takes all our sins away;
> a Sacrifice of nobler name
> and richer blood than they.[2]

Never underestimate the power of guilt and never underestimate the power of being set free from guilt. Guilt is one of the main sources of anxiety and anxiety is one of the main triggers for all the things we do to self-soothe, things that become addictive and destructive and that, in turn, make us feel even guiltier than before. To have that burden lifted from us is to experience a complete reset. The cycle is finally broken. The very appetite to do those things mysteriously evaporates. Our relationship with others is improved because we are no longer carrying a sense of indebtedness and inferiority. Consequently, we've no longer got something to prove about our worth and status. We are less defensive, more confident, and much more honest with people.

But not only does guilt cause us to live with a feeling of deficiency and debt, it creates a vague expectation of punishment. There is the feeling that judgment hangs over us, but we don't know what it will be or when it will come. Some people cannot bear the uncertainty of this so take matters into their own hands

2. Watts, "Not All the Blood of Beasts."

and punish themselves, perhaps with the very self-destructive behaviors that brought on the guilt in the first place. Indeed, suffering more guilt is part of the self-induced punishment. A self-induced punishment, after all, is preferred to a nonspecific, non-controllable punishment. Lift the guilt, and all this goes away!

Truly, there is "Power in the Blood."

REMAIN

> We know that Christ, being raised from the dead, will never die again; death no longer has dominion over him. For the death he died he died to sin, once for all, but the life he lives he lives to God.

Though yet to encounter our own deaths, we see from the deaths of others that no one ever comes back from that place. Death is *extremely final.* It severs every connection that the person once had with this life. Death, without any self-effort, severs all such relationships.

When we are bereaved, the loss is very final, but the grieving process happens in stages. Indeed, one of the stages of grief is denial. It takes awhile for us to understand and accept the finality of the loss. Participating in Holy Saturday is an unfolding finality. Something really has happened, but it requires a daily taking-up of the cross, a daily dying, a daily immersion into Christ and his death, to slowly bring into our lived experience the death that we have died. It slowly dawns on us that we are not what we were. In him we have truly died.

At this point, it is good to ask ourselves, who baptizes us into Christ? Is it the waters of baptism? Can water be that magical? First Corinthians 12:13 tells us that by one Spirit we were all baptized into the body of Christ. It is the Spirit who joins us to Christ and immerses us into him. And it is into Christ himself, not into water, that we are immersed. I have found great benefit in asking the Spirit, for several mornings in a row, to steep me in Christ, to saturate me in him. It is only as we discover ourselves to be in Christ that the newness of this life and the oldness of the old ways of being become clear. It's through the action of the Spirit steeping us in Christ that these things become real to us.

CONCLUSION

To be buried with Christ is a key part of the package. It is a state first entered by the door of the imagination. Once there, our faith can help us embrace and welcome that entombed reality. In the tomb with Jesus we find rest, and in the tomb we discover how free we are. And, though Sunday is coming, there is something of this rested state that we will carry with us. We will carry into the joy of risen life, a rested heart that has been freed from guilt and no longer needs what it once thought it needed.

9.

Session 4: John 15:4–5

A Fruitful Life

PARTS OF THIS SESSION have been adapted from a sermon I gave the very day after my own experience of my oneness with Christ. The audience included a number of guests who were the friends and relatives of a couple who were renewing their vows. There seemed to be especially rapt attention when I spoke about the life of Brother Lawrence.

> Abide in me, and I in you. As the branch cannot bear fruit by itself, unless it abides in the vine, neither can you, unless you abide in me. I am the vine; you are the branches. Whoever abides in me and I in him, he it is that bears much fruit, for apart from me you can do nothing. (John 15:4–5)

INTRODUCTION: LIFE HACKS

> Pleasing Sights: The sea, the night sky. Green plants. Well-chosen furniture and wall colors, clothing, tableware. Warm indoor lighting.
>
> Pleasing Sounds: Music of one's own choosing. Bird song, waves.

> Pleasing Scents: Flowers. Herbs and spices such as lavender, nutmeg, vanilla. The natural scent of certain healthy humans.
>
> Painful Sights: Slums and ghettos. Plastic toys. Institutional interiors, including hospital corridors, schools, and transportation hubs.
>
> Painful Sounds: Sirens, car horns, traffic. Other people's music. Dogs barking. Babies crying. Dripping water.

This is an extract from a list of things deemed pleasurable or painful for the senses, offered by a modern advocate of Epicureanism.[1] It forms part of an argument about self-care in which the readers are encouraged to enjoy themselves in simple, inexpensive ways. Such enjoyment comes by avoiding sensory pain, by, for instance removing "every plastic bottle, tube or jar with a written label from your line of sight in the bathroom or kitchen." Many other life hacks follow in which the reader is invited to eat well, avoid buying unnecessary things, and do things that one genuinely finds enjoyable, for example, learning an instrument not because you ought to but because you love it.

The aim of such advice is, of course, happiness. The aim is well-being, human flourishing, and the desire is that this would be an unperturbable, stable kind of happiness. We want real peace, not the fake kind we can get by being mildly intoxicated with our favorite cocktail. We want real joy, not merely the lift that comes from good coffee.

Any happiness guru will tell you that true happiness cannot be a wholly self-absorbed pursuit. It must involve connections with others, and it must involve having the chance to do things that seem worthwhile, things that give something back to our community.

The charity Action for Happiness includes "meaning" as number ten of its ten keys to happiness:

> People who have a sense of meaning in life tend to experience more frequent and stronger positive emotions;

1. Wilson, *Pleasure Principle*, 79–80.

> feel more positive about the future; have greater life satisfaction; have higher psychological wellbeing; have more satisfying relationships; use their character strengths more and feel better about themselves. Meaning in life is associated with physical health benefits such as reporting fewer ill-health symptoms, lower risk of heart disease, stronger immune systems and being less likely to engage in behaviours that undermine physical health. It also seems to help us live well for longer. People reporting higher meaning in life tend to have lower levels of physical and cognitive decline and live to an older age.[2]

Action for Happiness define meaning as "a sense of being connected to, part of, and/or contributing to something bigger, beyond ourselves."[3] They insist, however, that, "There's no single prescription to what meaning means in our own lives."[4] We are invited, instead, to brainstorm as many of the ways that we can think of in which we are already connected to people and nature and where we could already make a difference.

This is not a million miles away from very similar teachings given in Christian books, except Christian versions would not say that "there's no single prescription to what meaning means." They would work from the assumption that there is ultimately one fundamental thing that provides us with meaning, and that's faith.

John, and John's Jesus, seem to be working from a similar assumption, but their concept of what faith is might be quite surprising to many today. They think the answer to the sad human condition, the answer to our lack of happiness, is that there would be a bond, a connection, between God and humans that is so close it is interpenetrating. It involves, according to one recent study of John, the "dissolution of personal space,"[5] and "a presence so close and intimate it is portrayed as 'internal' to the life of the other."[6]

2. Action for Happiness, "Meaning."
3. Action for Happiness, "Meaning.
4. Action for Happiness, "Meaning.
5. Bowsher, *Life in the Son*, 51, citing Richard Bauckham, *Gospel of Glory*, 13.
6. Bowsher, *Life in the Son*, 51.

And then, through this interpenetrating union, access is given to "life," the life of the age to come in the here and now. And that is what faith is in John's Gospel.

The most in-depth explanation of this I-in-you-and-you-in-me level of connection is to be found in John 15:1–8. We will focus on verse 4: "Abide in me, and I in you."

THE HOW OF ABIDING

One of the persistent questions around this command to "abide" in Christ, is "How do I abide?" If we are told to stand up, sit down, walk around, do this, do that, we might resent being bossed around like that, but we at least know what to do. If we are told to "abide" we feel slightly stumped. We might want to obey the command, but we don't know *how* to obey it. Some clarification is needed.

In 1865 James Hudson Taylor founded the China Inland Mission (now OMF), and within just a few years found himself overwhelmed by success. He had pioneered a new method of mission, which no longer relied on a London-based mission board that would be variously out of touch with how things were on the ground. The China Inland Mission was based on the bold new idea that mission could proceed on the basis of pure faith and prayer, that the missionaries themselves, who were mostly working-class men and women, could be empowered to make their own decisions in situ, and local dress and customs would be adopted so that missionaries were no longer sequestered behind a compound, and, further, local people would be empowered to take part in the mission.

The mission grew to such a size so quickly that Taylor found himself becoming more and more aware of his own inner frailties as the strain showed itself. "My own position becomes continually more and more responsible," he wrote to his mother in 1869, "and my need greater of special grace to fill it; but I have continuously to mourn that I follow at such a distance and learn so slowly to imitate my precious Master."[7] Taylor had had some exposure to the Methodists' ideas about entire sanctification, and wondered whether there was yet some deeper work that God might do within him. He needed saving from himself. He struggled with an inner "unrest" and there was a constant pursuit of "some way by which I might continuously enjoy that communion, that fellowship at times so real, but more often so visionary, so far off!"[8]

He often corresponded with his sister Amelia about his meditations on the vine and the branches of John 15:1–8. However, his letter to her dated September 6, 1869, stands out. It tells of a life-changing breakthrough. It happened as a result of a visit from a certain Mr. McCarthy, who had himself just come into an experience of sanctification in Christ, with much help from the vine and branches passage, and had told Taylor all about it in a letter in which he explains how he sees the whole thing working. He quotes from a book that seemed to make it clear: "This [grace of faith] is the chain which binds the soul to Christ, and makes the Saviour and the sinner one . . . A channel is now formed by which Christ's fulness plenteously flows down. The barren branch becomes a portion of the fruitful stem . . . One life reigns throughout the whole.'"

Hudson Taylor writes excitedly to Amelia:

> Here, I feel, is the secret: not asking how I am to get sap *out* of the vine *into* myself, but remembering that Jesus *is* the Vine—the root, stem, branches, twigs, leaves, flowers, fruit, all indeed. Aye, and far more too! He is the soil and sunshine, air and rain—more than we can ask, think, or desire. Let us not then want to get anything out of him, but rejoice in being *ourselves in Him*—one with Him, and, consequently, with *all* his fulness.[9]

"One life reigns throughout the whole." Hudson Taylor's breakthrough came by seeing that Christ was all in all. The only fitting response was to rest in him and allow the life that is in the vine in such abundance to flow, via the faith channel, into the branch.

7. Taylor and Taylor, *Hudson Taylor and the China Inland Mission*, 166.
8. Taylor and Taylor, *Hudson Taylor and the China Inland Mission*, 168.
9. Taylor and Taylor, *Hudson Taylor and the China Inland Mission*, 172.

Not until our work flows out from this resting state can our work be fruitful. Until then, we are just busy; we bear lots of very attractive leaves, but no fruit. We got involved in lots of things that we once thought were meaningful. They would qualify under number ten in Action for Happiness's keys to happiness. But demand has outstripped supply and we are burning out. We need the Father's pruning.

But, aside from resting (which we already covered in our previous session), how do we maintain the *fruitfulness* of abiding in Christ? We want to stop the busyness but promote the fruitfulness. The fruit comes by faith like everything else, but Jesus gives us a hint about how we exercise that faith: "Ask whatever you wish, and it will be done for you. By this my Father is glorified, that you bear much fruit . . ." (John 15:7). Those that have seen any success at living a life of close and conscious union with Christ have tended to say much about prayer, and when they speak of prayer, they often envisage an act of faith that takes us far beyond the mere act of asking for things. Jesus clearly teaches that asking for things is the immediate basis of fruitfulness, but the very image of abiding compels us to look for a path of prayer that may have asking for things as its destination, but which practices deep communion all along the way. Prayer that begins in abiding communion bears fruit in the things it asks for.

Brother Lawrence of the Resurrection, whose birth name was Nicolas Herman (1614–91), was a "discalced," that is, barefoot, Carmelite monk. However, in earlier life he was a soldier. In that role he was twice injured during the Thirty Years' War. One of these injuries left him with a limp, which only added to his bungling awkwardness. He describes himself as a "great awkward fellow who broke everything."[10] After leaving the army he became a footman to an aristocratic family. But he wasn't very good at it. You guessed it, he kept breaking things. Finally, at the age of twenty-six, he joined a monastery in Paris, hoping that he could make himself useful there by performing some humble duty. Sure

10. An entire blog post is devoted to this self-designation: "Great Awkward Fellow Who Broke Everything."

enough, they set him to work in the kitchen, catering for about a hundred monks. Presumably, he carried on breaking things, but he must have made a mean stew, so they kept him on in that role. Poor Brother Lawrence never really enjoyed the set times of prayer in the day but what he did discover was that, even amid a busy kitchen with all the noise and sweat and demands being shouted at him, he could experience a powerful sense of the presence of God just by chatting affectionately with God. Indeed, he claimed that after twenty years of this, he could virtually "see" God: "I see him in a way which could at times make me say: 'I no longer believe, but see.' I experience what faith teaches us, and upon this assurance and practice of faith I shall live and die with him.'"[11]

When asked what he does if the presence of God seems to withdraw, he said he recovered it easily

> by a lifting of the heart, or by a sweet and loving gaze or by some words which love discovers in these encounters—as for example: "My God, here I am, all yours"; "Lord, fashion me according to thy heart." And then it appears to him [writes his biographer] that he experiences indeed that the God of love, satisfied with these few words, returns to rest and to repose in the very centre of his soul. The consciousness of these things makes him so aware that God is ever in the depths of his being, that he can conceive no doubt about it, whatever he does and whatever happens to him.[12]

If you would live a life of abiding, then prayer must no longer be limited to formalities or to a set time in the day. It must be a life in which we, to quote Paul, "Rejoice always, pray without ceasing, give thanks in all circumstances" (1 Thess 5:16–18).

The Orthodox have a strong tradition of attempting to live a life in which we breathe prayer, night and day. The great Russian classic *The Way of the Pilgrim* is a series of tales written about a journey to find the secret of unceasing prayer. The anonymous writer tells of a "staret," an elder or spiritual father of the church,

11. Lawrence, *Practice of the Presence of God*, 55.

12. Lawrence, *Practice of the Presence of God*, 35–36.

whom he met on his pilgrimage. The elder advised him to simply say the Jesus Prayer: "Lord Jesus Christ, have mercy on me." The writer found work for the summer guarding a garden so was free to devote every day to prayer. The staret began by advising the pilgrim to say the Jesus Prayer 3,000 times each day for a week, then come back and see him. Each week, the pilgrim doubled the number until, eventually, he was saying the prayer even in his sleep, without counting the number. He was saying it sometimes loudly, at other times quietly, or silently. It often seemed to match the beating of his heart. The more he did this, the more joy he found: "I have become a sort of halfwit, I have no cares, nothing preoccupies me, I wouldn't spare any worldly thing a glance . . ."[13]

Whatever method is chosen, prayer must begin in a way that secures this continuous fellowship. Then, as we ask what we desire we start to bear fruit. Asking is what happens once deep fellowship has been aroused. Bold requests erupt from a heart alive to the nearness of God. And these requests, according to the passage, are requests directed at the Father. A pattern in John's Gospel is that the Spirit's passion is to show us Christ and glorify him, but Christ desires to introduce us to the Father. It is, after all, the Father that is glorified in our bearing much fruit and the Father who is the vine-dresser. It is the Father-centricity of the Son that prevents our union with Christ from being a thing that only confirms our subjectivization. It is a union that points Father-ward, an immanence that ushers us toward transcendence. The Father then becomes our refuge, in place of the refuges we once sought. He becomes the one in whom we learn what it means to be still and know that he is God. We give glory and honor to him in our adoration. And then we find ourselves wearing his glory, and whatever we ask the Father in Christ's name, he gives to us (John 15:16).

13. Anonymous, *Way of the Pilgrim*, 14.

THE FRUIT OF ABIDING

Jesus promises "much fruit." The Greek for "much" is *polus*, which means often repeated. If we abide in him we are able to bear this fruit again and again without burning out. But what exactly did Jesus have in mind as the fruit of abiding and asking?

There are two options. On the basis of what follows not long after this verse, bearing much fruit is the effect on our daily life of being in union with Christ.[14] It is the life of loving self-sacrifice that is described in John 15:9–16. And it is at the end of this section about loving self-sacrifice that Jesus again uses the image of fruit-bearing, which rather seems to confirm our hunch that this is what he means by fruit: "You did not choose me, but I chose you and appointed you that you should go and bear fruit and that your fruit should abide" (John 15:16).

However, you'll have noticed that Jesus includes the word "go." There seems to be a sense of mission entering in here. And this leads us to the second option.[15] All the way back in John 4:34–38, Jesus speaks of fields white for harvest, which seems to be about people entering the kingdom, and in John 12:24 we have the same phrase "bear much fruit," though this, as in John 4, is to do with a cereal crop rather than grapes. Jesus likens his impending death to an ear of wheat that must fall to the ground if it is to bear much fruit. In 12:32, that fruit would appear to be all the people that will be drawn to him as a result of his death on the cross.[16] So, whereas the first option—the fruit of loving self sacrificial discipleship—was about what comes *after* our vine-and-branches passage, this missional take on the fruit relies on what went *before* this passage.

So, is it the fruit of being good disciples, or the fruit of winning others?

John's Gospel seems to give commentators moments like this all the time. A classic example is "Lamb of God" in John 1:29 and 36. Scholars ask, does this mean the Passover lamb, Jesus brings

14. Brown, *John XIII–XXI*, 665; Carson, *John* 2, 511.

15. Bolt, "What fruit does the vine bear," 16.

16. Bolt, "What fruit does the vine bear," 16.

a new exodus, or is it the lamb led to the slaughter of Isaiah 53:7? Or does this mean *lamb* as symbolic of all the animals that could be offered as sin offerings in Leviticus: Jesus is the sin-bearer? Or does John the Baptist mean *lamb* as symbolizing gentleness (cf. Jeremiah 11:19)? Another example is the "Word" of John 1:1. Is this the Word of Isaiah 55:11, the Word that does not return void but accomplishes what God pleases, or is it the Word of Greek Stoicism, the Logos, the animating intelligence that sustains all things? Often scholars are left concluding that John's writings are full of multiple meanings. The way John writes is deceptively simple. He likes straightforward opposites like truth and lies, darkness and light, and so we think he is not nuanced or complex or deep. Then, as we ponder his writings, we realize there are untold depths and a whole spread of meanings. Likely, we can take fruit to mean that the fruit of good discipleship, which if it is growing healthily, will reproduce itself, will propagate itself. It's both-and.

CONCLUSION

Happiness is impossible without meaning, and meaning, as we've seen, is "a sense of being connected to, part of, and/or contributing to something bigger, beyond ourselves." This is precisely the picture of the vine and the branches. Each branch is connected to the far bigger thing of Christ himself and all that he is doing in the world today. As we connect to him, we find ourselves involved with what he is involved with. It is "the presence of each party in the life of the other."[17] It is what has been referred to as a "mutual mind state." In such a state, "we cannot consciously be sure which are our thoughts and feelings and which come from the beloved other."[18] As a result of hosting his life in us, we think his kind of thoughts, make his kind of requests in prayer, and bear his kind of fruit, meaningful fruit.

17. Bowsher, *Life in the Son*, 51.

18. Wilder and Willard, *Renovated*, 38. I'm indebted to PhD student Abigail Clayton for locating this.

Happily, the only way to bear this kind of fruit is to nestle into this union. It is an interpenetrating, personal-space obliterating, but deeply satisfying oneness with the being we were all along made to be one with. Such intimacy, such "reciprocal immanence"[19] satisfies the deepest longings of our hearts.

19. Bowsher's translation of a key phrase in Jerumanis, *Réaliser la communion avec Dieu*, 358 : Bowsher, *Life in the Son*, 16. The phrase is "d'immanence réciproque."

Conclusion

In this book I have been making the claim that, rather than defining Western culture using one of the popular "isms," which tend to be too reductionistic, "Epicureanism" (though also an "ism") may be more useful. The term gives us as preachers and teachers a thick description of a range of recurring cultural traits, some of which we can quite readily make positive connections with, especially in view of the fact that Epicureanism formed a significant part of the context in which the New Testament itself was written, so that we get to see there some worked examples of how the gospel and Epicurean culture can connect.

One of these connection points is the Epicurean pursuit of true happiness. Happiness is the realization of *ataraxia*, the absence of disturbance and trouble, the lack of any fear. I have shown some of the ways in which the good news of Christ shows the way to the realization of that pursuit. I am putting forward an in-one-another participative view of the work of Christ as the gospel we should preach in an Epicurean age. It draws upon the this-worldly emphasis the New Testament itself uses when appealing to probable Epicurean-influenced audiences.[1] Not that modern Epicureanism is in every way a perfect fit for the participation-in-Christ gospel. Today's Epicureanism is founded, like its ancient counterpart, on a materialistic view of the universe that gives rise to a religiously

1. It also draws upon the deeply rooted biblical equation between the presence of God and the absence of any reason therefore to be afraid (Deut 31:6,8; Josh 1:5; Pss 27:1; 118:6). And fear was understood by Epicurus, as well as today's thinkers, to be enemy number one of true happiness and peace.

indifferent disposition and a deeply individuated pursuit of happiness. My claim is simply that there is an access point. We can enter by way of our shared interest in well-being. And the immanent starting point—Christ in *me*—does not even demand of the Epicurean that they renounce their individualism. It transforms it into something less lonely. And it is a union that does, in the end, deliver us from our self-orientation, as the Christ to whom we are united introduces us to the Father and to his people.

Our message leaves untouched any indifference toward the kind of religion that claims the moral high ground, or which is all about where we go when we die, or which keeps God at a deistic distance (Christian Smith's "moralistic therapeutic deism"). People now are mostly not fully atheist but are *religiously* apathetic. The ancient Epicureans were hostile toward what they called "popular religion." Today's Epicureans have an issue with "organized religion," the kind that "causes all the wars." Our culture is deeply suspicious of a phenomenon that is supposed to know its place as a privately held set of convictions but instead keeps becoming "organized" and therefore a threat. Our gospel's sole interest is Christ, toward whom indifference has always been a near impossible option.

But why the long history lesson? Why did I need to include such an extensive survey of Christian history? After all, the Greek fathers and the Byzantines were not advocating theosis in the context of an especially Epicurean culture—it was on the wain by then. And by the golden age of Catholic mysticism, the dominant worldview in European Christendom was Christian Platonism—the exact opposite of what we know in the Epicurean Age. Even at the time of the holiness movements, although Epicurean atomism had left its mark, we were still yet to see the universal quest for self-actualized well-being that predominates today. So, it's not as if these eras give us lessons about how preaching union-with-Christ to Epicureans "worked" back then and could work again today. What can be said is that, if these participative understandings of the gospel were understood to be the answer to the human condition in the enchanted Platonic Age, how much more so during the howling spiritual semi-desert that is the Epicurean Age. The need today has only become greater.

Somebody once said that although we all use different terms for it, union with Christ is the one major doctrine that all the major confessional blocs agree on. We have all seen the same truth—and it is perhaps the only aspect of Christian doctrine of which that can be said. The central importance of a living and vital union with Christ is the one undisputed truth. This fact is something that has fascinated me since I first came across it. My historical survey hopefully highlights the way this one agreed-on central aspect of the life of faith has summoned forth some of the very best theological and devotional writings of all time.

Lastly, though I talk of an Epicurean culture, the message I have in mind is not necessarily "evangelistic." In my four sessions much of the content could be seen as aimed at Christians. The issue is that the Epicurean values of our culture are to be found almost as much within the church as outside it. The gospel is for the poor within and without the church.

I hope this book reminds us of the uniqueness of the offer that is the gospel. It has been said countless times before, but it is clearer than ever to me that Christianity is not just another religion. Its message offers us something that was meant to be the ultimate antidote to religion, as well as the way to lasting happiness and peace. There is nothing like this message, and too little of it has been preached for too long.

Besides continuing to preach and teach this message, what I plan to do next, seeing as I am an artist by background, is engage again in the world of creatives. I am building up a portfolio of paintings with a view to reviving my earlier profession. And this might be my last nonfiction book as I seek ways of using creative writing to connect with a culture that's mostly not very interested in the books I've written so far.

May God's hand be with you as you reach out in whatever sphere you find yourself sent to.

"Here I am, send me" (Isa 6:8).

Bibliography

Action for Happiness. "Meaning." https://actionforhappiness.org/10-keys/meaning.

Aldis, W. H. *The Message of Keswick and its Meaning.* London: Marshall, Morgan & Scott, n.d.

Anatalios, Khaled. *Deification through the Cross: An Eastern Theology of Salvation.* Grand Rapids: Eerdmans, 2020.

Anonymous. *The Way of the Pilgrim: Candid Tales of a Wanderer to His Spiritual Father.* Translated by Anna Zaranko. London: Penguin, 2017.

Aston, Katie. "United Kingdom: All Publicity is Good Publicity, Probably." In *The Atheist Bus Campaign: Global Manifestations and Responses,* edited by Steven Tomlins and Spencer Cuəlham Bullivant, 334–68. Leiden: Brill, 2017.

Athanasius. *Athanasius de Incarnatione: An Edition of the Greek Text.* Edited by Frank Leslie Cross. Eugene, OR: Wipf & Stock, 1963.

———. "Letter to Adelphium 4." In *Nicene and Post-Nicene Fathers* 4, edited by Philip Schaff, 576. New York: Christian Literature, 1892.

Augustine of Hippo. *Confessions.* Translated by R. S. Pine-Coffin. London: Penguin, 1961.

Bailey, George. "Growing into God: A Consideration of the Relation Between the Experience and Theology of Sanctification, in Dialogue with John Wesley's Theology of Perfection and Gregory Palamas' Theology of Deification." PhD diss., University of Oxford, 2010.

Bauckham, Richard. *Gospel of Glory: Major Themes in Johannine Theology.* Grand Rapids: Baker Academic, 2015.

Bebbington, David. "Holiness in the Evangelical Tradition." In *Holiness Past and Present,* edited by Stephen Barton, 298–315. Edinburgh: T & T Clark, 2003.

Bernard of Clairvaux. *Love Without Measure.* Translated by P. Diemer. London: Darton, Longman & Todd, 1990.

———. *On the Song of Songs.* Vol. III. Translated by Killian Walsh and Irene M. Edmonds. Piffard, NY: Cistercian, 1979.

Bettenson, Henry, ed. *The Early Christian Fathers*. Oxford: Oxford University Press, 1956.

Boardman, William. *The Higher Christian Life*. New York: Appleton, 1859.

Bolt, Peter. "What fruit does the vine bear: Some pastoral implications of John 15:1–8." *The Reformed Theological Review* 51:1 (January–April 1992) 11–19.

Bowsher, Clive. *Life in the Son: Exploring Participation and Union with Christ in John's Gospel and Letters*. London: Apollos, 2023.

Brown, Colin. *Philosophy and the Christian Faith*. Downer's Grove, IL: InterVarsity, 1969.

Brown, Raymond. *The Gospel According to John XIII–XXI*. New Haven: Yale University Press, 2013.

Bruce, F. F. *Commentary on the Book of Acts*. Grand Rapids: Eerdmans, 1981.

Bultmann, Rudolf. *Essays Philosophical and Theological*. London: SCM, 1955.

———. *Theology of the New Testament II*. London: SCM, 1955.

Carson, Don. *The Gospel According to John*. Vol. 2. Grand Rapids: Eerdmans, 1991.

Cary, Philip. "The Mythic Reality of the Autonomous Individual." *Zygon* 46:1 (March 2011) 121–34.

Casanova, Jose. *Public Religions in the Modern World*. Chicago: University of Chicago Press, 1994.

Cavanaugh, William. "'A Fire Strong Enough to Consume the House': The Wars of Religion and the Rise of the State." *Modern Theology* 11:4 (1995) 397–420.

———. *The Myth of Religious Violence: Secular Ideology and the Roots of Modern Conflict*. Oxford: Oxford University Press, 2009.

Cell, George Croft. *The Rediscovery of John Wesley*. New York: Henry Holt, 1935.

Christensen, Michael J., and Jeffery Wittung, eds. *Partakers of the Divine Nature: The History and Development of Deification in the Christian Traditions*. Grand Rapids: Baker Academic, 2008.

Cicero. *Tusculan Disputations*. https://www.gutenberg.org/files/14988/14988-h/14988-h.htm.

Corrigan, Kevin. "Mysticism in Plotinus, Proclus, Gregory of Nyssa, and Pseudo-Dionysius." *The Journal of Religion* 76:1 (January 1996) 28–42.

De Lubac, Henri. *The Drama of Atheist Humanism*. San Francisco: Ignatius, 1995.

Edwards, Aaron. "Secular Apathy and the Public Paradox of the Gospel: Towards Radical Inculturated Proclamation." *International Journal of Public Theology* 3:4 (December 2019) 413–31.

Fassetta, Raffaele. "The Christocentric and Nuptial Mysticism of Saint Bernard." *Cistercian Studies Quarterly* 49:3 (2014) 347–65.

Finlan, Stephen, and Vladimir Kharlamov, eds. *Deification in Christian Theology, Volume One*. Eugene, OR: Wipf and Stock, 2006.

Franks, R. S. *The Atonement*. Oxford: Oxford University Press, 1933.

Gavriluk, Paul. "The Retrieval of Deification: How a Once-Despised Archaism Became an Ecumenical Desideratum." *Modern Theology* 25:4 (October 2009) 647–59.

Goltitzin, A. *St Symeon the New Theologian: On the Mystical Life: The Ethical Discourses.* New York: St Vladimir's Seminary Press, 1996.

"A Great Awkward Fellow Who Broke Everything." Medium, June 13, 2024. https://medium.com/the-dove/a-great-awkward-fellow-who-broke-everything-c1d537b534b8.

Gregory of Nazianzus, *The Five Theological Orations of Gregory of Nazianzus.* Edited by Arthur Mason. Cambridge: Cambridge University Press, 1899.

Gregory Palamas "Those who practise a life of stillness 7." In *The Philokalia: The Complete Text* 2, translated by G. E. H. Palmer, Philip Sherrard, and Kallistos Ware, 285–305. London: Faber & Faber, 1981.

Grubb, Norman. *Once Caught, No Escape.* Cambridge: Lutterworth, 1969.

Guyon, Jeanne. *Experiencing the Depths of Jesus Christ.* Jacksonville, FL: SeedSowers, 1975.

Hampton, Alexander, and John Kenney, eds. *Christian Platonism: A History.* Cambridge: Cambridge University Press, 2021.

Hanover, Jacqui. "The Role of the Spiritual Senses in Contemporary Mission with Particular Reference to John Wesley's Employment of the Spiritual Senses: A Revised Correlational Approach." PhD thesis, University of Manchester, 2018.

Harrison, Anna. "'Jesus Wept': Mourning as Imitation of Christ in Bernard's Sermon Twenty-Six on the Song of Songs." *Cistercian Studies Quarterly* 48:4 (2013) 433–67.

Heelas, Paul, and Linda Woodhead. *The Spiritual Revolution: Why Religion is Giving Way to Spirituality.* Oxford: Wiley, 2005.

Heitzenrater, R. P., ed. *The Works of John Wesley.* 27 vols. Nashville: Abingdon, 1970—.

Hill, Jonathan. *The History of Christian Thought.* Oxford: Lion, 2003.

Hindmarsh, Bruce. *The Evangelical Conversion Narrative: Spiritual Autobiography in Early Modern England.* Oxford: Oxford University Press, 2009.

Hobbes, Thomas. *Leviathan.* Oxford: Oxford University Press, 1998.

Holder, Arthur, ed. *Christian Spirituality: The Classics.* London: Routledge, 2009.

Hutchinson, D. S., ed. *The Epicurus Reader: Selected Writings and Testimonia.* Cambridge: Hackett, 1994.

Ian A. McFarland, "'Naturally and by grace': Maximus the Confessor on the operation of the will." *Scottish Journal of Theology* 58:4 (2005) 410–33.

Irenaeus. *Against Heresies. Sources Chrétiennes no. 153: Irénée de Lyon: Contre Les Hérésies Livre V.* Paris: Les Éditions Du Cerf, 1969.

Jerumanis, Pascal-Marie. *Réaliser la communion avec Dieu: Croire, vivre et demeurer dans l'Evangile selon S. Jean.* Études Bibliques 32. Paris: Peeters, 1996.

Jiang, Shuguang, Qian Wei, and Luyao Zhang. "Individualism vs. Collectivism and the Early-Stage Transmission of COVID-19." *Research Gate*. https://www.researchgate.net/figure/Collectivism-vs-individualism-world-map-Note-The-colored-tape-in-the-right-part-of-the_fig7_342782204.

Jones, C., G. Wainwright, and E. Yarnold, eds. *The Study of Spirituality*. London: SPCK, 2000.

Jones, E. Stanley. *Victory Through Surrender: Self-Realization Through Self-Surrender*. Oxford: Abingdon, 1966.

Jungkuntz, Richard. "Christian Approval of Epicureanism." *Church History* 31:3 (1962) 279–93.

King, Fergus. *Epicureanism and the Gospel of John*. Tübingen: Mohr Siebeck, 2020.

Laertius, Diogenes. *Lives of Eminent Philosophers* Books 6–10. Translated by R. D. Hicks. Cambridge: Harvard University Press, 1931.

Lawrence, Brother. *Practice of the Presence of God*. Translated by E. M. Blaiklock. London: Hodder & Stoughton, 1990.

Lee, Bo Karen. "Madam Jeanne Guyon (1648–1717) *A Short and Very Easy Method of Prayer*." In *Christian Spirituality: The Classics*, edited by Arthur Holder, 257–68. London: Routledge, 2009.

Lossky, Vladimir. *The Mystical Theology of the Eastern Church*. London: James Clarke, 1991.

Louth, Andrew. *Maximus the Confessor*. London: Routledge, 1996.

———. *The Origins of the Christian Mystical Tradition: From Plato to Denys*. Oxford: Oxford University Press, 2007.

Lucretius. *On the Nature of Things*. Translated by Cyril Bailey. Oxford: Clarendon, 1910.

Luibheid, Colm. *Pseudo-Dionysius: The Complete Works*. New York: Paulist, 1987.

Luther, Martin. *D. Martin Luthers Werke: kritische Gesammtausgabe* 120 vols. Weimar: Hermann Böhlau, 1883–1929.

———. *Galatians* (Wheaton: Crossway, 1998), 106.

Lyotard, Jean-Francois. *The Postmodern Condition: A Report on Knowledge*. Translated by Geoffrey Bennington and Brian Massumi. Manchester: Manchester University Press, 1984.

Macleod, Donald. *The Person of Christ*. Leicester: Inter-Varsity, 1998.

Maddox, Randy. *Responsible Grace: John Wesley's Practical Theology*. Nashville: Abingdon, 1994.

Matthews, Rex. "'Religion And Reason Joined:' A Study In The Theology Of John Wesley." PhD diss., Harvard University, 1986.

Maximus the Confessor. *Centuries on Theology and the Incarnate Dispensation*. Extract Translated by Andrew Louth, *Maximus the Confessor*, 42. London: Routledge, 1996.

———. *Difficulty 10*. Translated by Andrew Louth. In *Maximus the Confessor*, 94–152. London: Routledge, 1996.

———. "Four Hundred Texts on Love." In *The Philokalia: The Complete Text* 2, translated by G. E. H. Palmer, Philip Sherrard, and Kallistos Ware, 53–113. London: Faber & Faber, 1981.

———. "Letter 2 On Love." Translated by Andrew Louth. In *Maximus the Confessor,* 84–93. London: Routledge, 1996.

———. *On Difficulties in Sacred Scripture: The responses to Thalassios. The Fathers of the Church: A New Translation, vol. 136.* Translated by Fr. Maximos Constas. Washington, DC: Catholic University of America Press, 2018.

———. "On the Lord's Prayer." In *The Philokalia: The Complete Text* 2, translated by G. E. H. Palmer, Philip Sherrard, and Kallistos Ware, 285–305. London: Faber & Faber, 1981.

Mayes, Andrew. *Celebrating the Christian Centuries.* London: SPCK, 1999.

McCartney, Jenny. "They're Really, Really Spiritual—That is, Totally Selfish." *Sunday Telegraph,* November 7, 2004. https://www.telegraph.co.uk/comment/columnists/jennymccartney/3612709/Theyre-really-really-spiritual-that-is-totally-selfish.html.

McCormick, Steve. "Theosis in Chrysostom and Wesley: An Eastern Paradigm on Faith and Love." *Wesleyan Theological Journal* 26 (1991)38–103.

McFarland, Ian A. "'Naturally and by grace': Maximus the Confessor on the operation of the will." *Scottish Journal of Theology* 58:4 (November 2005) 410–33.

McGinn, Bernard. "Love, Knowledge, and Mystical Union in Western Christianity: Twelfth to Sixteenth Centuries." *Church History* 56 (1987) 7–24.

Milbank, John. *Theology and Social Theory: Beyond Secular Reason.* 2nd ed. Oxford: Blackwell, 2006.

Nee, Watchman. *The Life That Wins.* New York: Christian Fellowship, 1986.

———. *The Normal Christian Life.* Eastbourne: Kingsway, 1961.

———. *Sit, Walk, Stand.* Eastbourne: Kingsway, 1977.

Neyrey, Jerome. "The Form and Background of the Polemic in 2 Peter." *Journal of Biblical Literature* 99:3 (1980) 407–31.

"Nominalism in Metaphysics." *Stanford Encyclopedia of Philosophy Archive.* https://plato.stanford.edu/archives/spr2025/entries/nominalism-metaphysics.

Nugent, Donald. "What has Wittenberg to do with Avila?" *Journal of Ecumenical Studies* 23:4 (Fall 1986) 650–58.

Outler, Albert. *John Wesley.* New York: Oxford University Press, 1964.

Palamas, Gregory. "Those who practise a life of stillness 7." In *The Philokalia: The Complete Text,* vol. 4, translated by G. E. H. Palmer, Philip Sherrard, and Kallistos Ware, 331–42. London: Faber and Faber, 1995.

———. *The Triads.* Translated by Nicholas Gendle. Ramsey, NJ: Paulist, 1983.

Palmer, G. E. H., Phillip Sherrard, and Kallistos Ware, eds. *The Philokalia: The Complete Text.* Vol. 4. London: Faber and Faber, 1995.

Palmer, Phoebe. *Faith and its Effects, or, Fragments from my Portfolio.* London: Alexander Heylin, 1856.

Penn-Lewis, Jessie. *The Cross of Calvary.* Poole: Overcomer, n.d.

———. *More Than Conquerors.* Poole: Overcomer, n.d.

Pickstock, Catherine. *After Writing: On the Liturgical Consummation of Philosophy.* Oxford: Wiley, 1997.

Plato. *Phaedo.* In *Plato: Complete Works,* translated by John Cooper, 49–100. Indianapolis: Hackett, 1997.

———. *Phaedrus.* Translated by G. P. Gould. Cambridge, MA: Harvard University Press, 1914.

———. *The Republic Books 6–10.* In *Plato: The Complete Works.* Edited by John Cooper. Indianapolis: Hackett, 1997

———. *Symposium.* In *Plato: The Complete Works,* edited by John Cooper, 457–505. Indianapolis: Hackett, 1997.

———. *Theaetetus.* Translated by Harold North Fowler. Cambridge, MA: Harvard University Press, 1921.

———. *Timaeus.* Translated by R. G. Bury. Cambridge, MA: Harvard University Press, 1929.

Price, Charles, and Ian Randall. *Transforming Keswick: The Keswick Convention Past, Present and Future.* Carlisle: Paternoster, 2000.

Pseudo-Dionysius. *The Complete Works.* Edited by Colm Luiheid. Mahwah, NJ: Paulist, 1987.

Pugh, Ben. *The Old Rugged Cross: A History of the Atonement in Popular Christian Devotion.* Eugene, OR: Cascade, 2016.

———. *One with Christ.* Eugene, OR: Cascade, 2023.

———. *Pictures of Atonement.* Eugene, OR: Cascade, 2020.

———. "Plato and His Big Idea: The Theory of Forms." *Dialogue: A Journal of Religion and Philosophy* 55 (November 2020) 9–13.

Radice, Betty. *The Letters of Abelard and Heloise.* London: Penguin, 1974.

Raffaele, Fassetta. "The Christocentric and Nuptial Mysticism of Saint Bernard." *Cistercian Studies Quarterly* 49:3 (2014) 347–65.

Ranocchia, Graziano. "Moses Against the Egyptian: Anti-Epicurean Polemic in Philo." In *Philo and Post-Aristotelian Philosophy,* edited by F. Alesse 75–102. Leiden: Brill, 2008.

Rodriguez-Pereyra, Gonzalo. "Nominalism in Metaphysics." *The Stanford Encyclopedia of Philosophy* (Summer 2019 Edition), Edward N. Zalta , ed. https://plato.stanford.edu/archives/sum2019/entries/nominalism-metaphysics/

Root, Andrew. *Faith Formation in a Secular Age.* Grand Rapids: Baker Academic, 2017.

Runyon, Theodore. *The New Creation: John Wesley's Theology Today.* Nashville: Abingdon, 1998.

Russell, Norman. *The Doctrine of Deification in the Greek Patristic Tradition.* Oxford: Oxford University Press, 2005.

Sayers, Dorothy L. *The Greatest Drama Ever Staged.* London: Hodder and Stoughton, 1938.

Schnabel, Eckhard. "Contextualising Paul in Athens: The Proclamation of the Gospel Before Pagan Audiences in the Graeco-Roman World." *Religion and Theology* 12:2 (2005) 172–90.

Simson, Wolfgang. *Houses That Change the World.* Milton Keynes: Authentic, 2001.

Smith, Christian. *Soul Searching: The Religious and Spiritual Lives of American Teenagers.* New York: Oxford University Press, 2005.

Smith, James K. A. *How (Not) to be Secular: Reading Charles Taylor.* Grand Rapids: Eerdmans, 2014.

Staniforth, Trevor. *The Methodist Pentecost: Personal Testimonies and Eyewitness Accounts of Revival in the 1760's and the Doctrine of Entire Sanctification.* Ilkeston: Moorley's, 2010.

Strodach, George, ed. *Epicurus: The Art of Happiness.* London: Penguin, 2012.

Synan, Vinson. *The Pentecostal-Holiness Tradition.* Grand Rapids: Eerdmans, 1997.

Szymik, Stefan. "The Corinthian Opponents of the Resurrection in 1 Cor 15:12. The Epicurean Hypothesis Reconsidered." *The Biblical Annals* 10:3 (2020) 437–56.

Tannehill, Robert. *Dying and Rising with Christ: A Study of Pauline Theology.* Eugene, OR: Wipf and Stock, 2006.

Taylor, Dr. and Mrs. Howard. *Hudson Taylor and the China Inland Mission.* Singapore: OMF, 1989.

Teresa of Avila, *The Interior Castle.* 3rd ed. Translated by The Benedictines of Stanbrook. London: Thomas Baker, 1921.

Thompson, Ross. *The SCM Study Guide to Christian Spirituality.* London: SCM, 2006.

Tomlin, Graham. "Christians and Epicureans in 1 Corinthians." *Journal for the Study of the New Testament* 68 (1997) 51–72.

Tournier, Paul. *Guilt and Grace.* Crowborough: Highland, 1986.

Truglia, Craig. "Highlights of Maximus' *Ambigua.*" https://orthodoxchristiantheology.com/2020/20/05/highlights-of-maximus-ambigua-to-john/.

Tyson, Paul. *Returning to Reality: Christian Platonism for Our Times.* Eugene, OR: Cascade, 2014.

Upham, Thomas. *Life, Religious Opinions and Experience of Madam de la Mothe Guyon.* New York: Harper & Brothers, 1877.

Vishnevskaya, Elena. "Divinization and Spiritual Progress in Maximus the Confessor." In *Theosis: Deification in Christian Theology*, edited by Stephen Finlan and Vladimir Kharlamov, 134–45. Eugene, OR: Pickwick, 2006.

Vladimir Lossky. *The Mystical Theology of the Eastern Church.* Cambridge: James Clarke, 1991.

Warfield, B. B. *Studies in Perfectionism.* Phillipsburg, NJ: Presbyterian and Reformed, 1961.

Watts, Isaac. "Not All the Blood of Beasts." 1709. *Hymnary.org.* https://hymnary.org/text/not_all_the_blood_of_beasts.

Wesley, John. "An Earnest Appeal to Men of Reason and Religion." In *The Works of John Wesley Vol. 8: Addresses, Essays, and Letters.* Edited by Thomas Jackson. London:Wesleyan Methodist Book-Room, 1872.

———. *A Plain Account of Christian Perfection.* London: Epworth, 1952.

White, C. E. *The Beauty of Holiness: Phoebe Palmer as Theologian, Revivalist, Feminist, and Humanitarian.* Grand Rapids: Francis Asbury, 1986.

Whittall Smith, Hannah. *The Christian's Secret of a Happy Life.* Grand Rapids: Baker, 1952.

Wilder, Jim, and Dallas Willard. *Renovated: God, Dallas Willard, and the Church that Transforms.* Colorado Springs: NavPress, 2020.

Wilson, Bill. *Alcoholics Anonymous.* New York: Alcoholics Anonymous World Services, 1939.

Wilson, Catherine. *Epicureanism at the Origins of Modernity.* Oxford: Oxford University Press, 2008.

———. *The Pleasure Principle: A Philosophy for Modern Living.* London: HarperCollins, 2019.

Winter, DeeDee. "Norman P. Grubb—History." https://normangrubb.com/home.

Index

www.ingramcontent.com/pod-product-compliance
Lightning Source LLC
LaVergne TN
LVHW090523110826
845146LV00003B/961

* 9 7 9 8 3 8 5 2 3 7 0 5 0 *